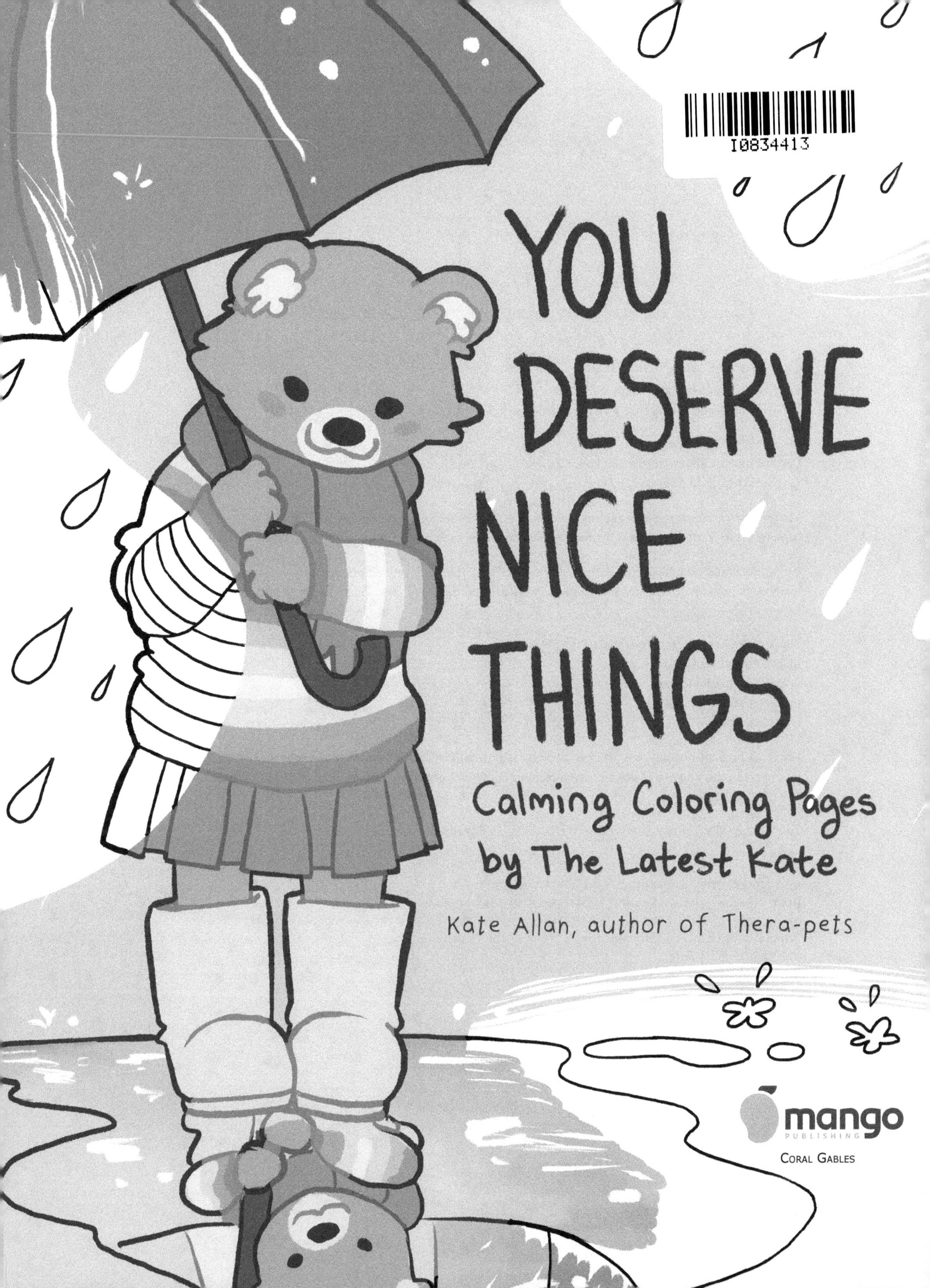
I0834413
YOU DESERVE NICE THINGS
Calming Coloring Pages by The Latest Kate
Kate Allan, author of Thera-pets
mango
PUBLISHING
Coral Gables

Published by Mango Publishing, a division of Mango Publishing Group, Inc.

Cover Design: Kate Allan
Cover + Interior Photo/illustration: Kate Allan
Layout & Design: Elina Diaz

For permission requests, please contact the publisher at:
Mango Publishing Group
2850 S Douglas Road, 4th Floor
Coral Gables, FL 33134 USA
info@mango.bz

For special orders, quantity sales, course adoptions and corporate sales, please email the publisher at sales@mango.bz. For trade and wholesale sales, please contact Ingram Publisher Services at customer.service@ingramcontent.com or +1.800.509.4887.

You Deserve Nice Things: Calming Coloring Pages by TheLatestKate

ISBN: (print) 978-1-64250-913-7 , (ebook) 978-1-64250-914-4
BISAC category code GAM019000, GAMES & ACTIVITIES / Coloring Books

Printed in the United States of America

This book belongs to:

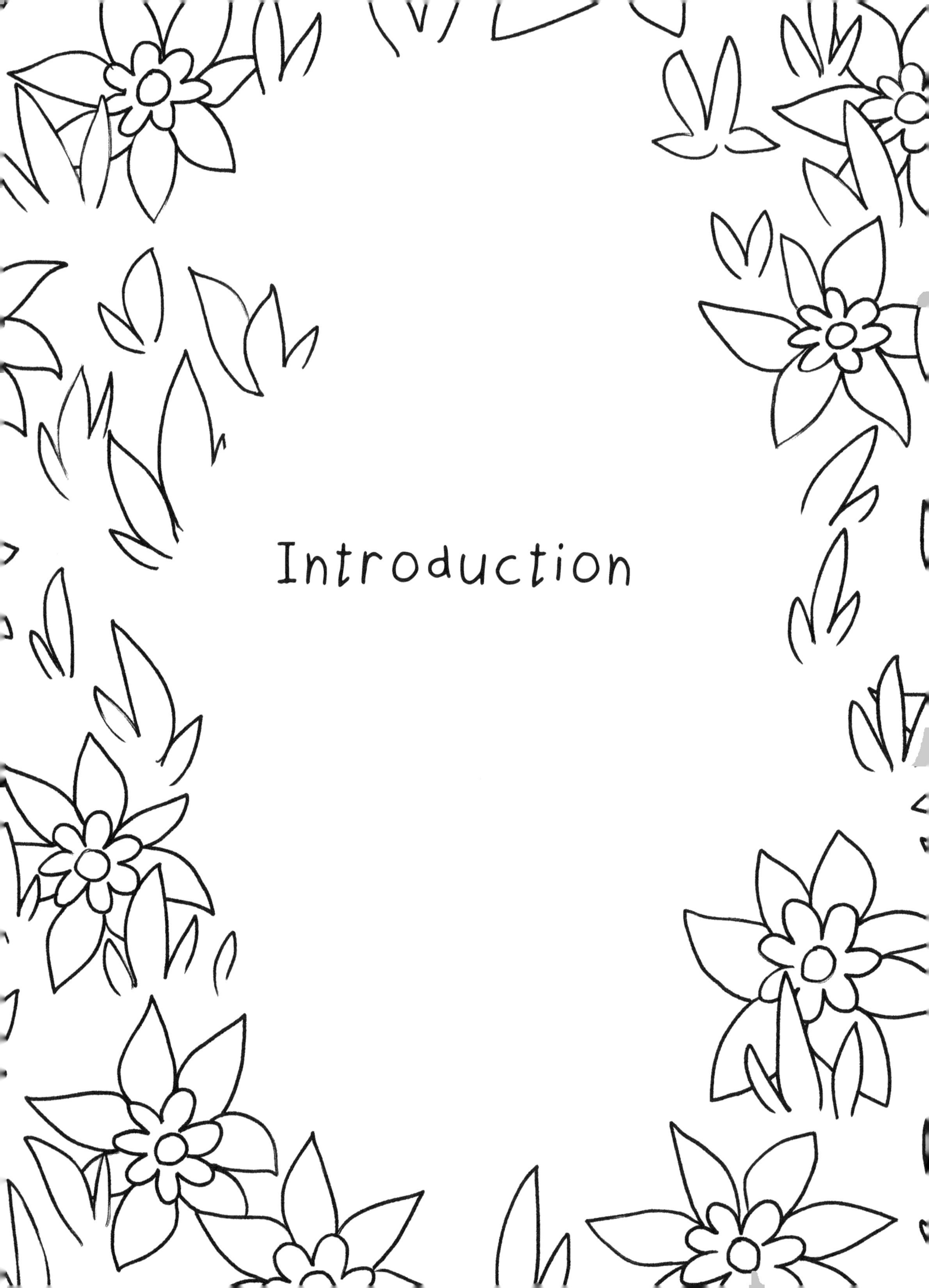

Introduction

Hello Colorist,

Thank you very much for picking up this coloring book! I hope you don't mind me sharing my story with you.

Since I was very young, I've had a very loud and persistent inner critic, who often told me incredibly unkind things. Most of my life, while trying to function normally and do things like pay attention in school, play games with friends, or finish my tasks at work, my inner critic consistently observed that I was unlovable, unworthy, unlikeable, taking up too much space, and a host of other cruel and unfounded ideas.

In response to this, I attempted a "fake it 'til you make it" approach where I tried to behave as normally as I could while simultaneously ignoring both the inner critic and how awful I felt. Unfortunately, as I aged and my problems grew to be more and more overwhelming, my goal of ignoring all my inner turmoil resulted in abysmally low self-esteem, a lack of direction in life, and several breakdowns.

In my mid-twenties, I fortunately was able to see a very kind therapist who recognized that I struggled with an inner critic. She suggested that I journal to argue against this negative, cruel inner voice as often as I could. It then became my goal to argue against these thoughts and judgements daily. Every time I felt tense, worried, sad, angry, overwhelmed, or filled with self-disgust or self-loathing, I dove into my journal and tried to look at my problems, thoughts, and feelings objectively. I then discovered a pattern; my distress was often triggered by a legitimate problem or fear, which I usually didn't know immediately how to deal with, and my inner critic would go to town by telling me I was deficient in various ways. This unchecked mental abuse caused me to feel uncontrollably awful. So, instead of continuing to stew daily in a quagmire of mental distress, I began a writing ritual of validating my struggles, accepting all of my emotions, and giving myself little pep talks.

After journaling for a few months, I found a magical pairing for myself; I'd always loved to draw and color, and pairing my daily writings with animals helped the messages to feel more potent. Somehow hearing these kindnesses and arguments from a colorful furry or feathered friend was more effective for my mind than just words on a page alone.

So here we find ourselves! My hope is that you can find some of your own solace and self-acceptance in coloring your way through this book. And if that doesn't happen, please at least know that you're not facing your life struggles alone. There are many of us out here quietly trying alongside you.

Cheering you on,
Kate Allan

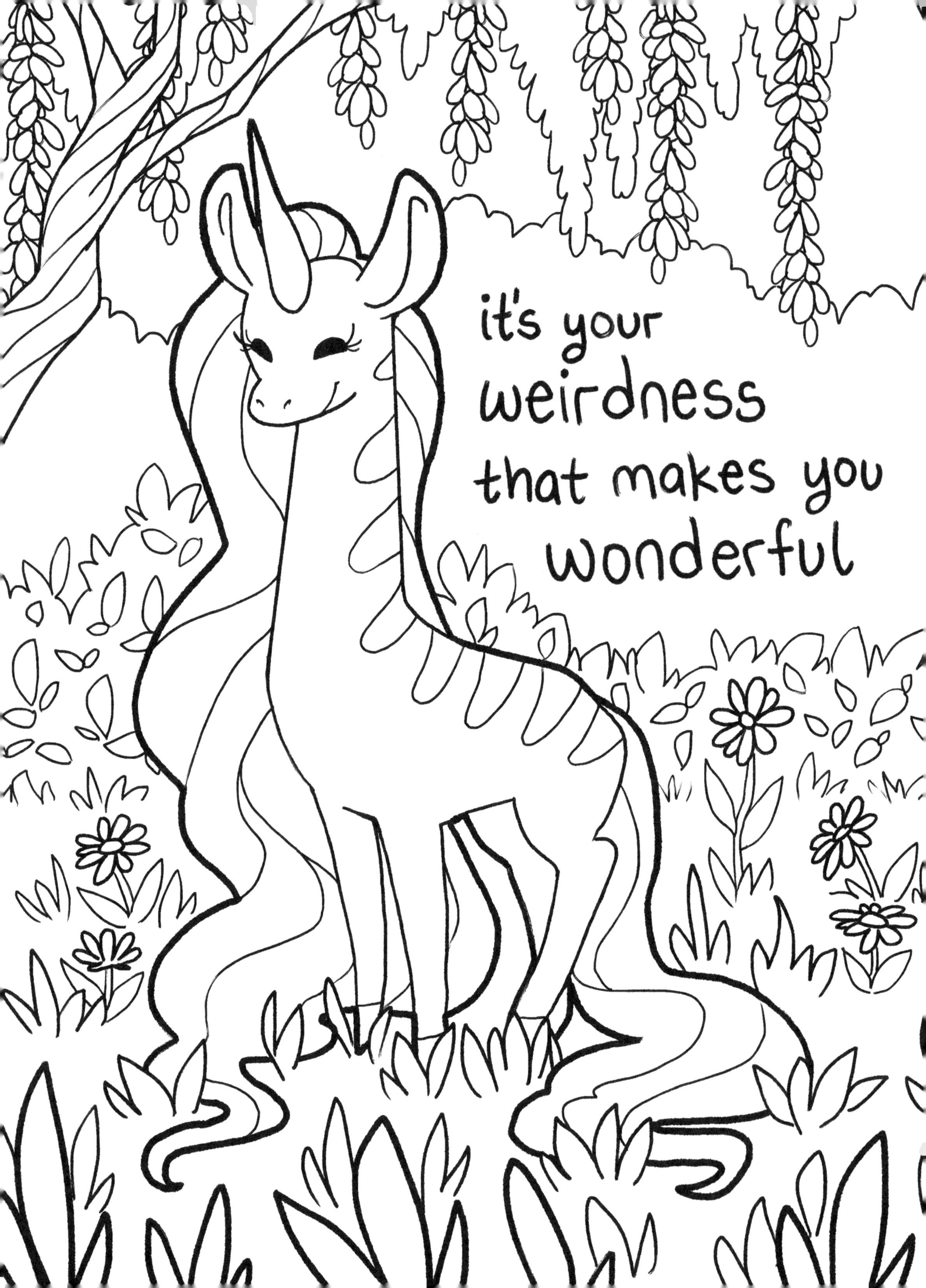
it's your
weirdness
that makes you
wonderful

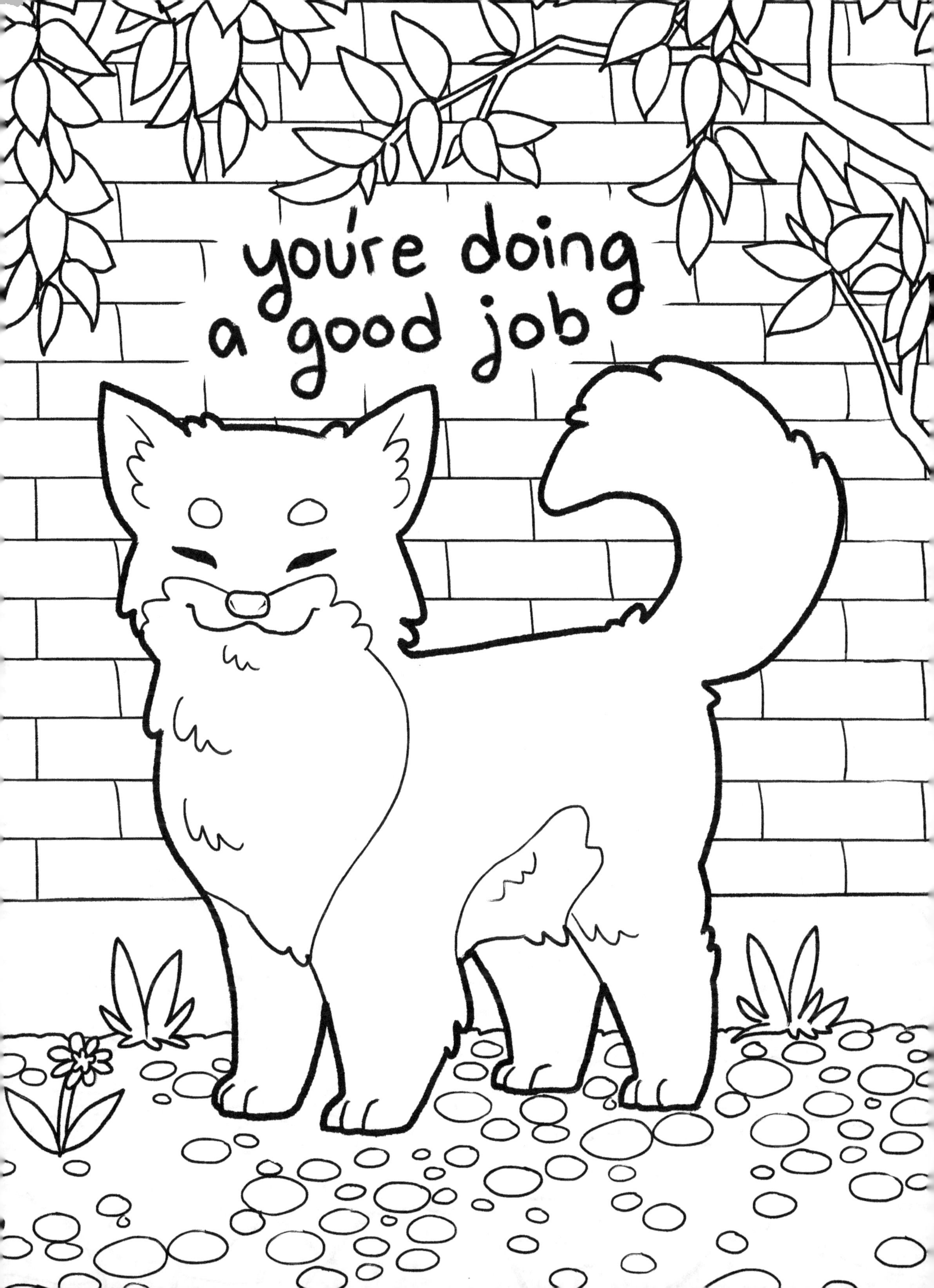
you're doing
a good job

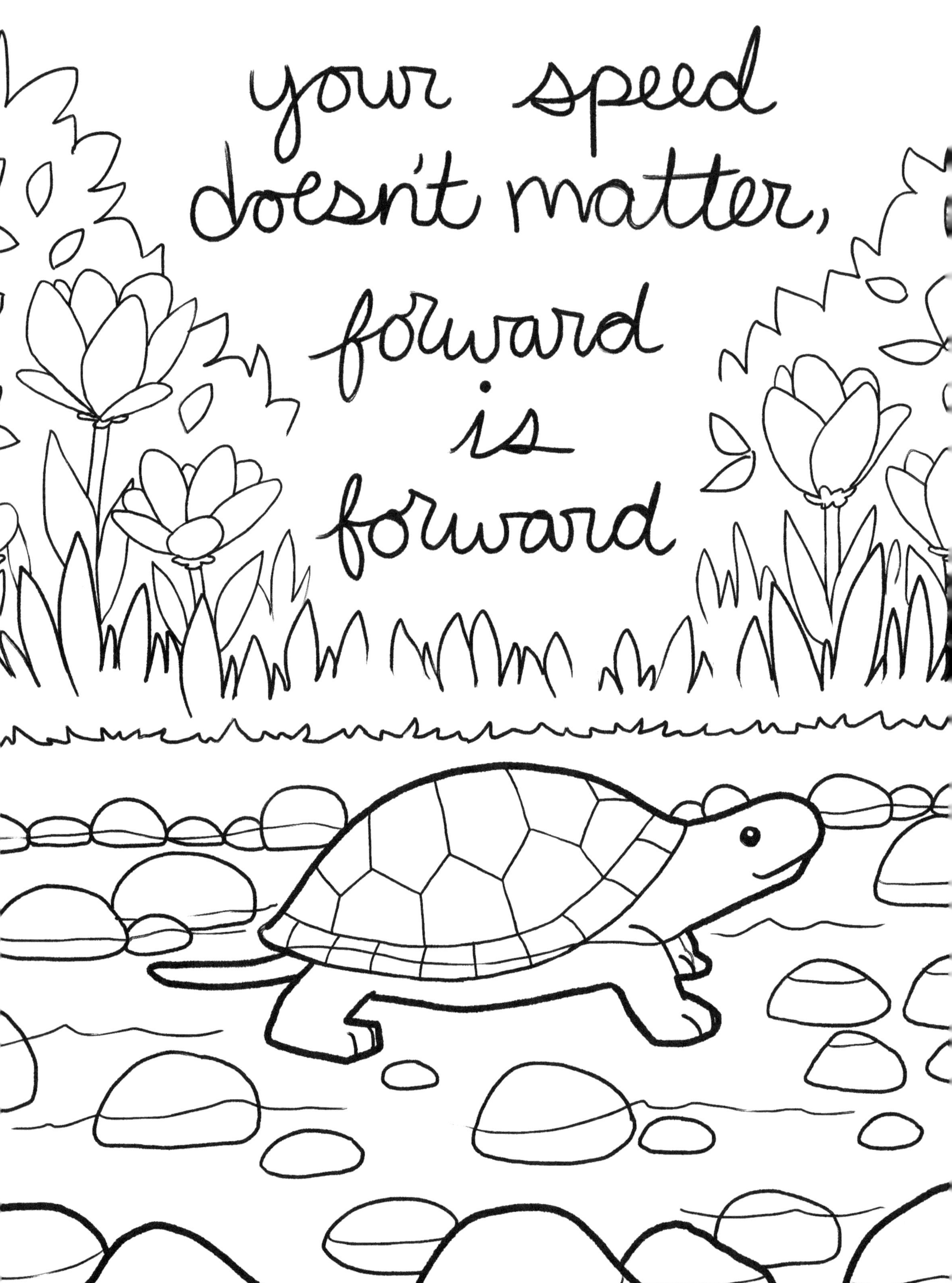
your speed
doesn't matter,
forward
is
forward

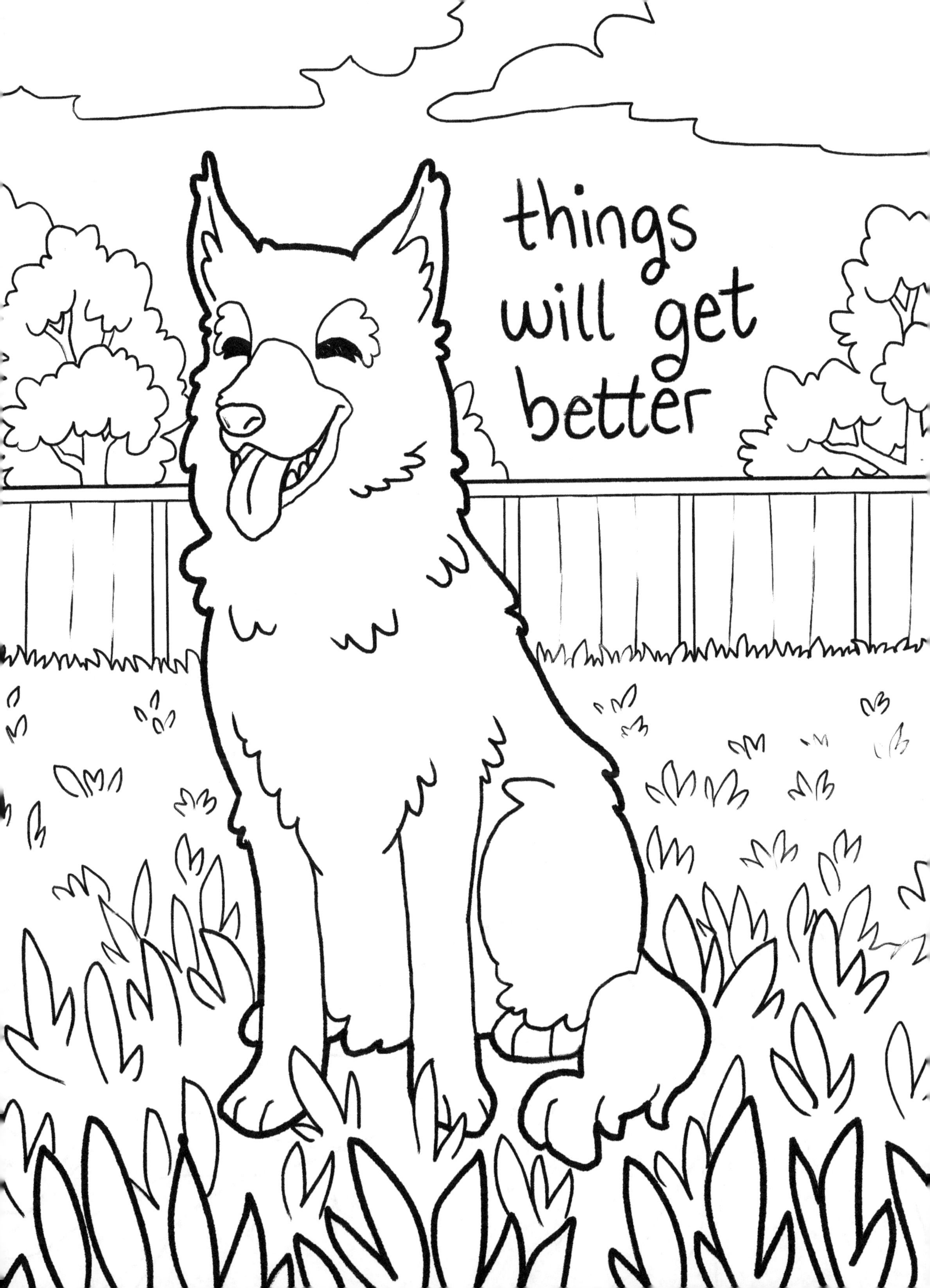
things
will get
better

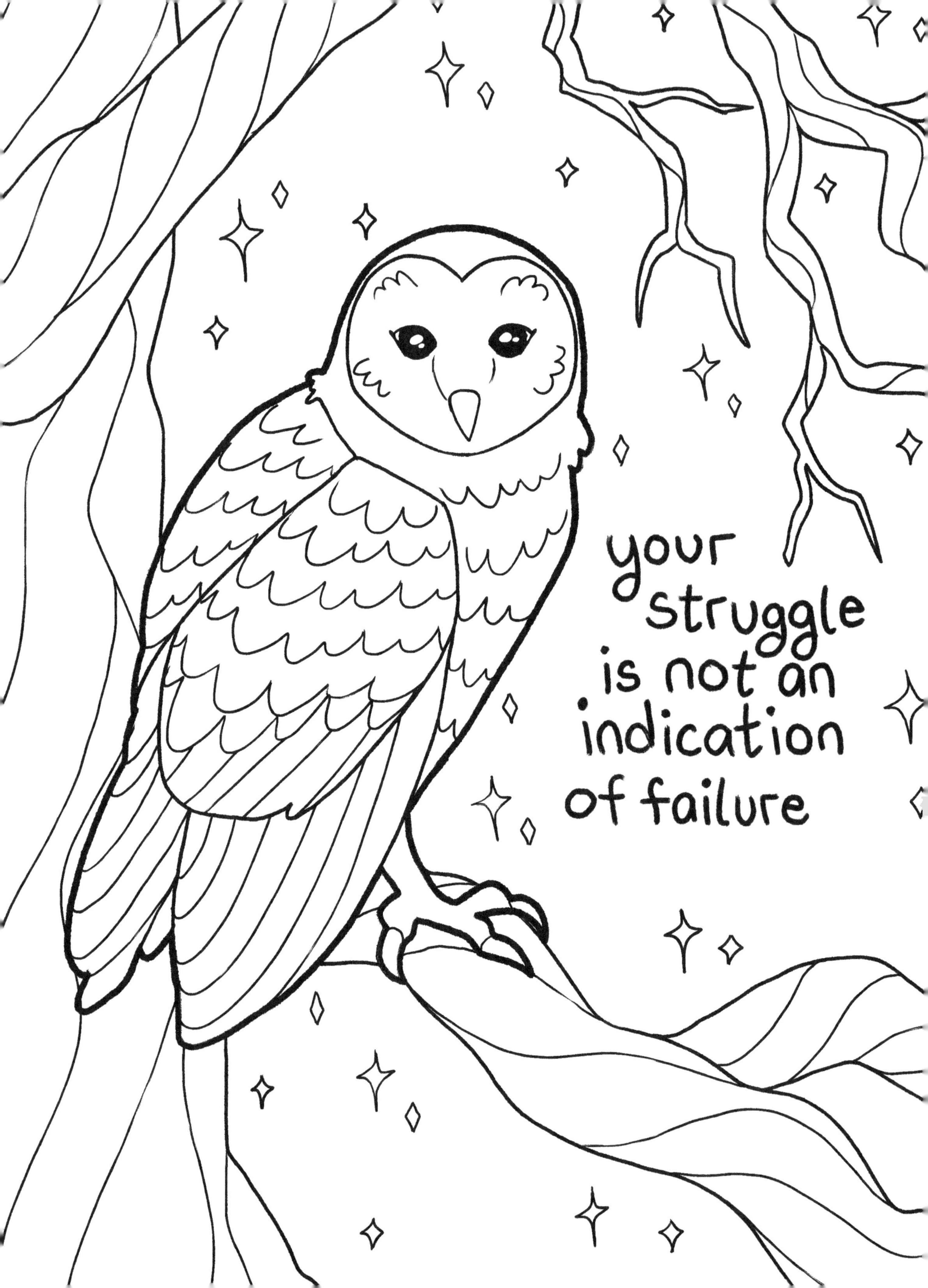
your
struggle
is not an
indication
of failure

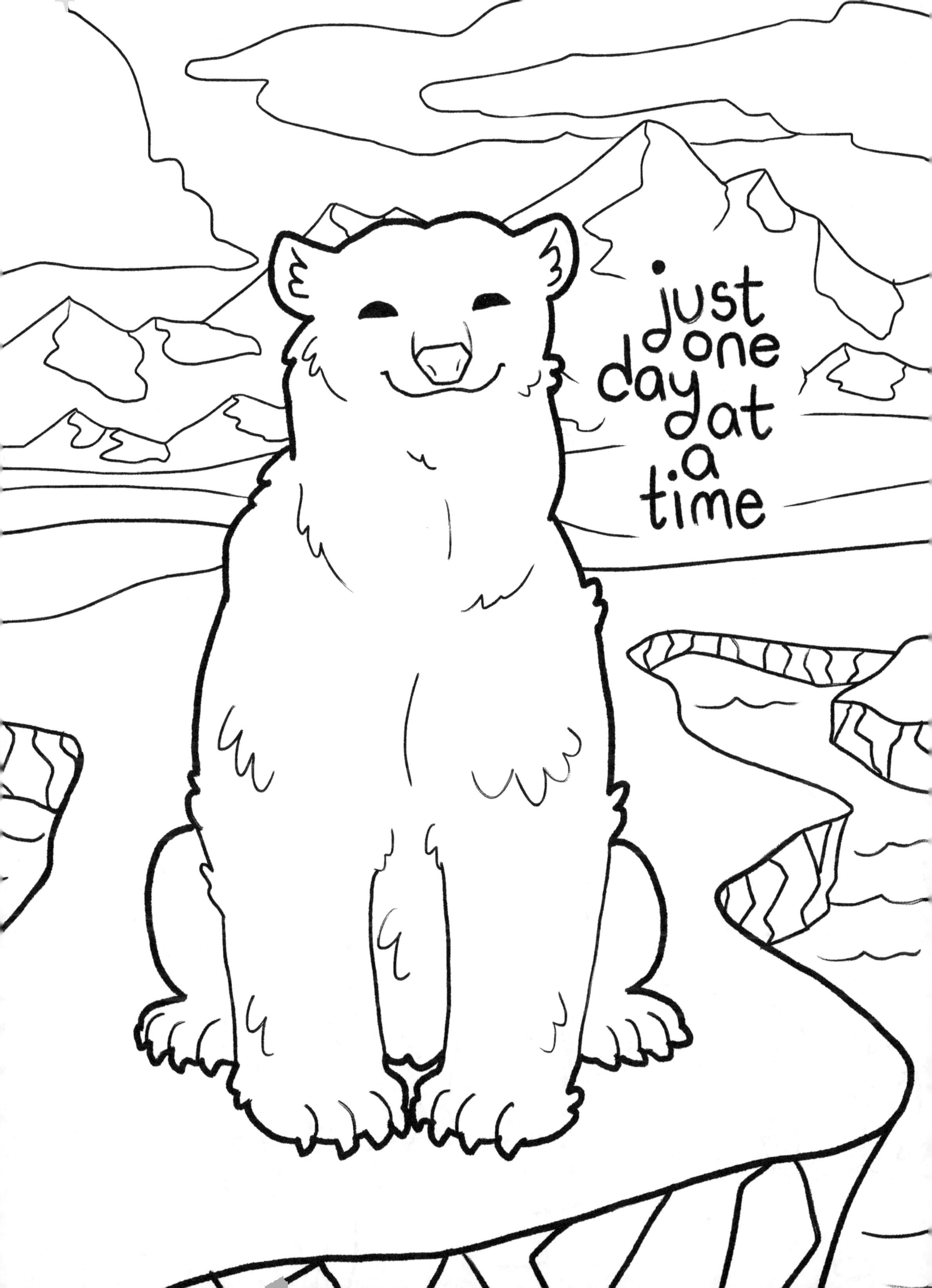
just one day at a time

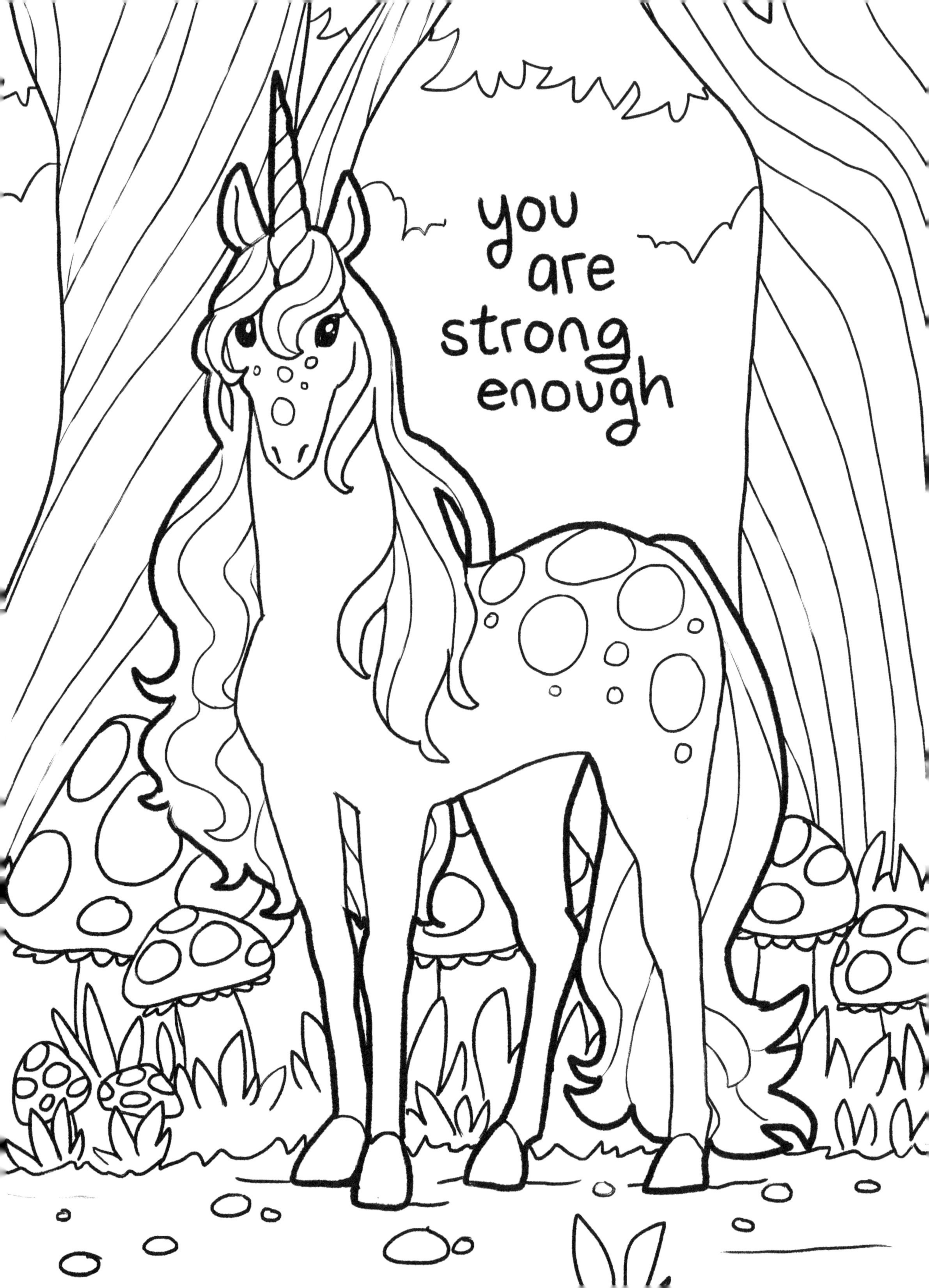
you
are
strong
enough

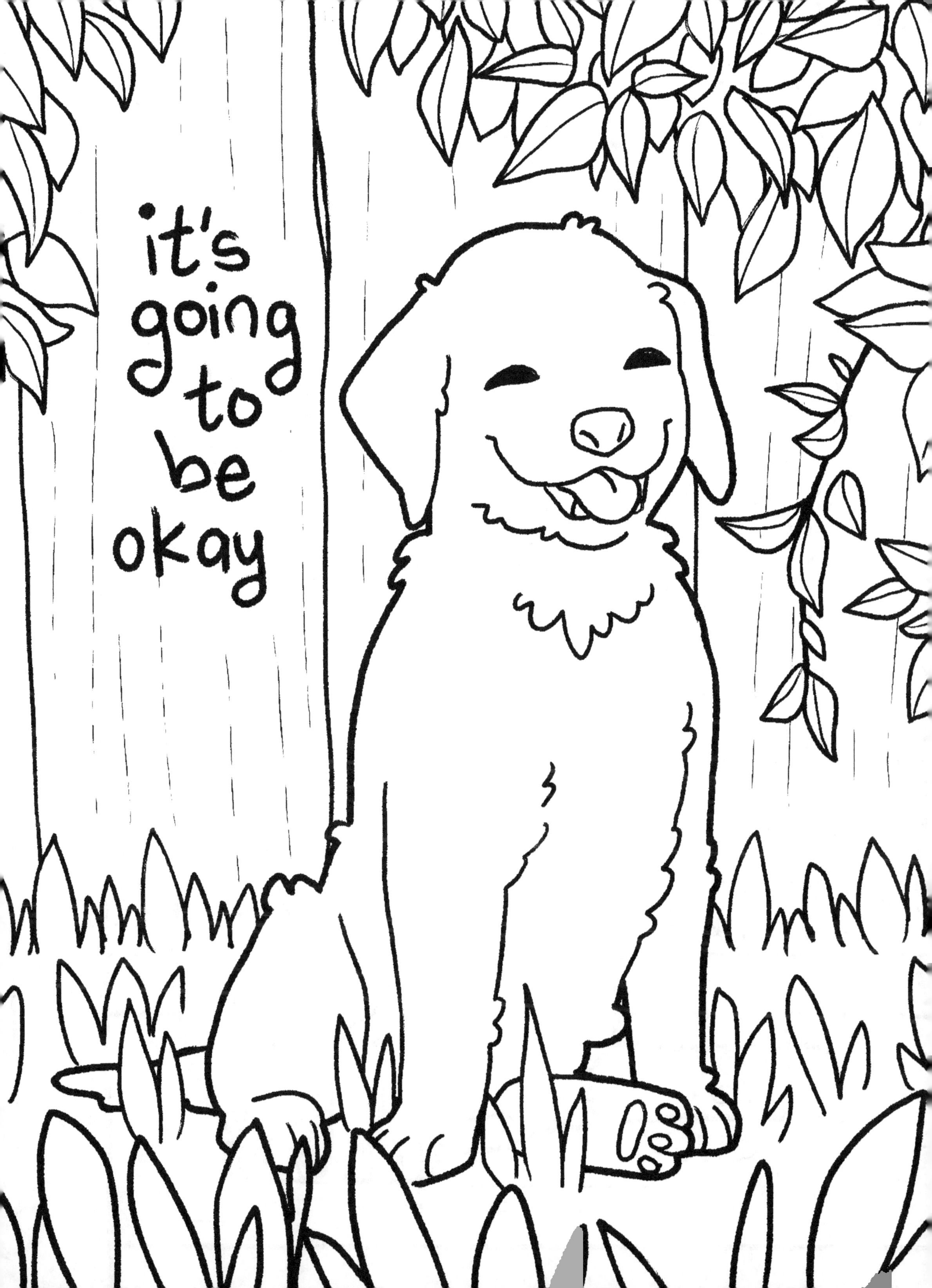
it's
going
to
be
okay

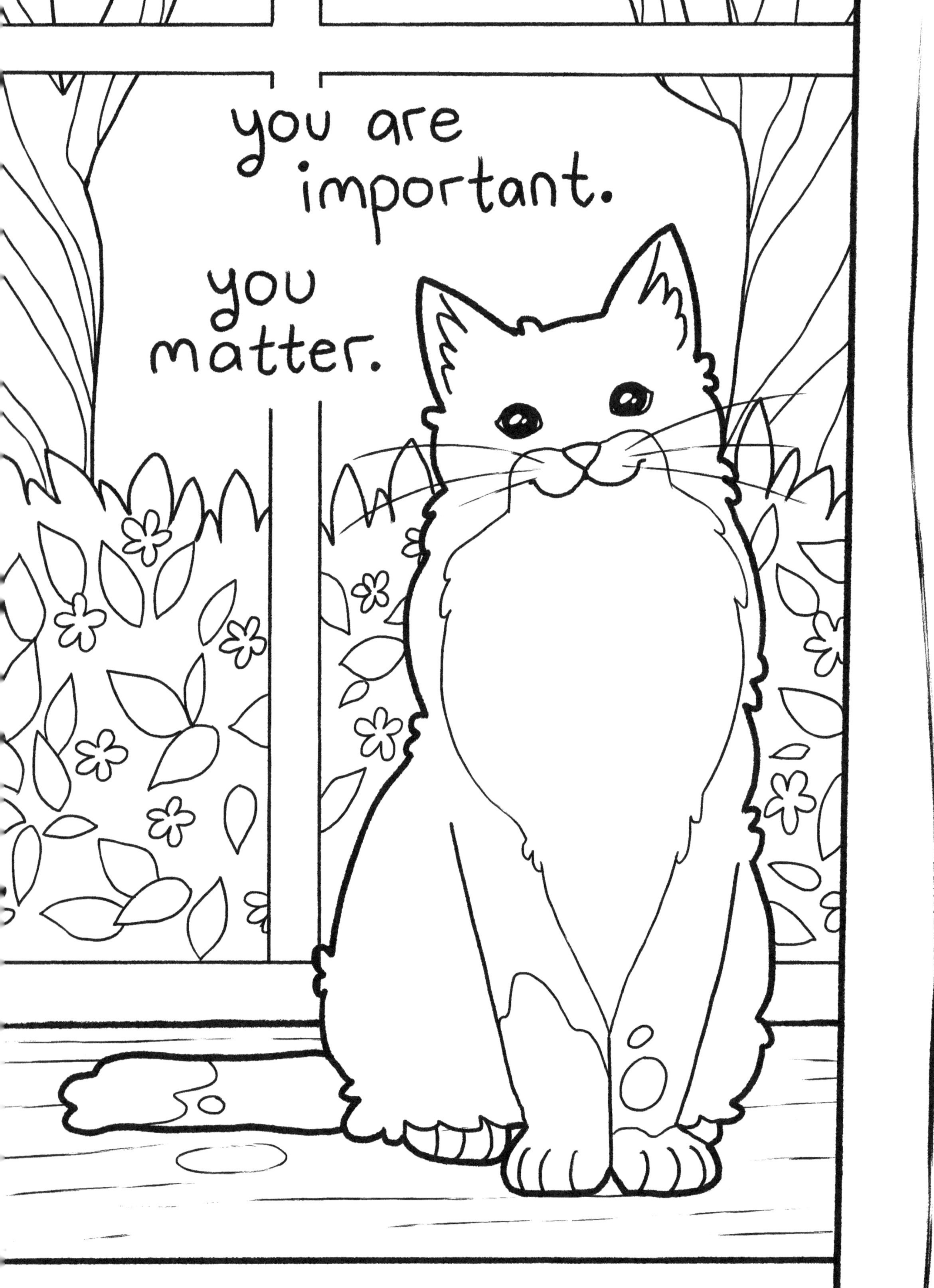
you are
important.
you
matter.

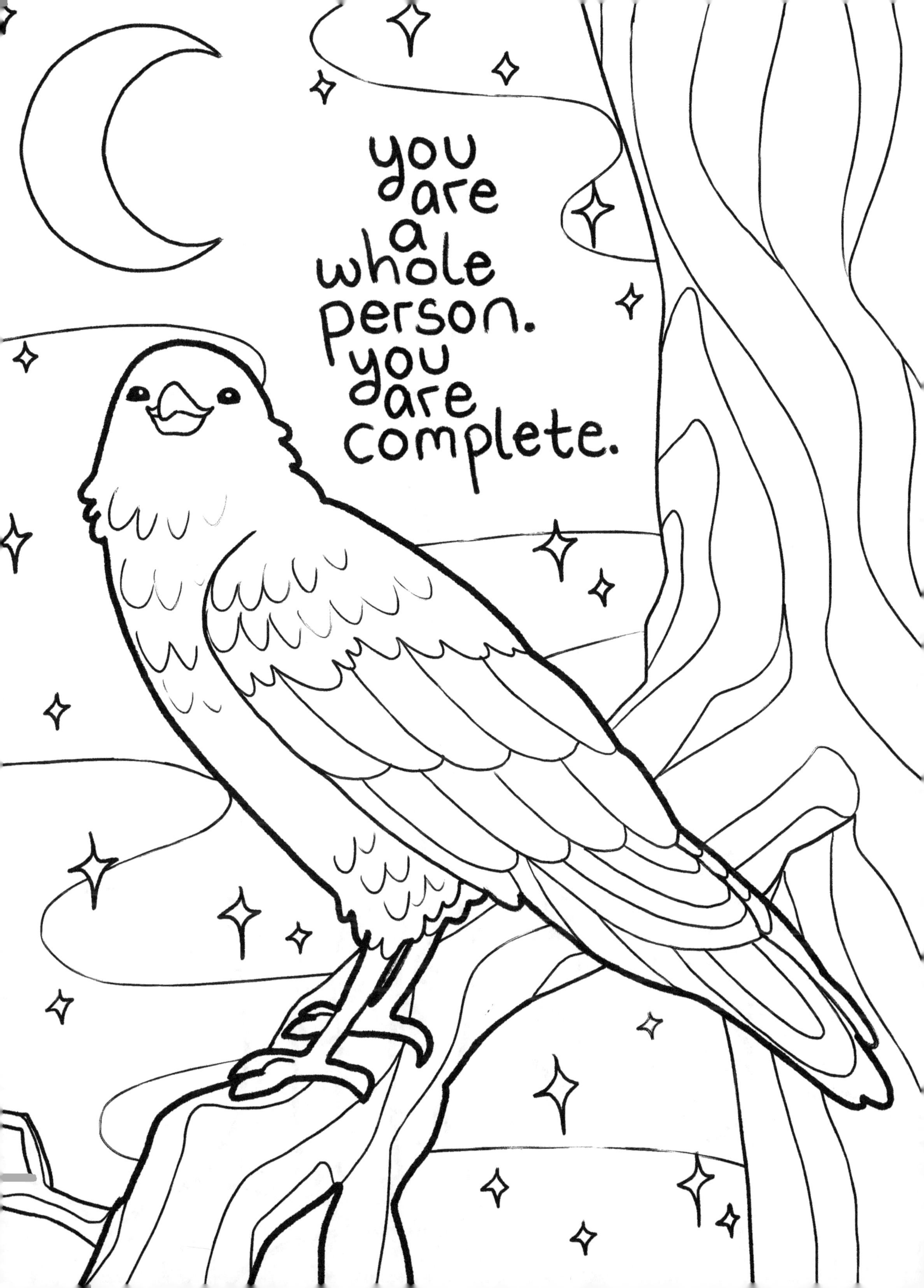
you are a whole person. you are complete.

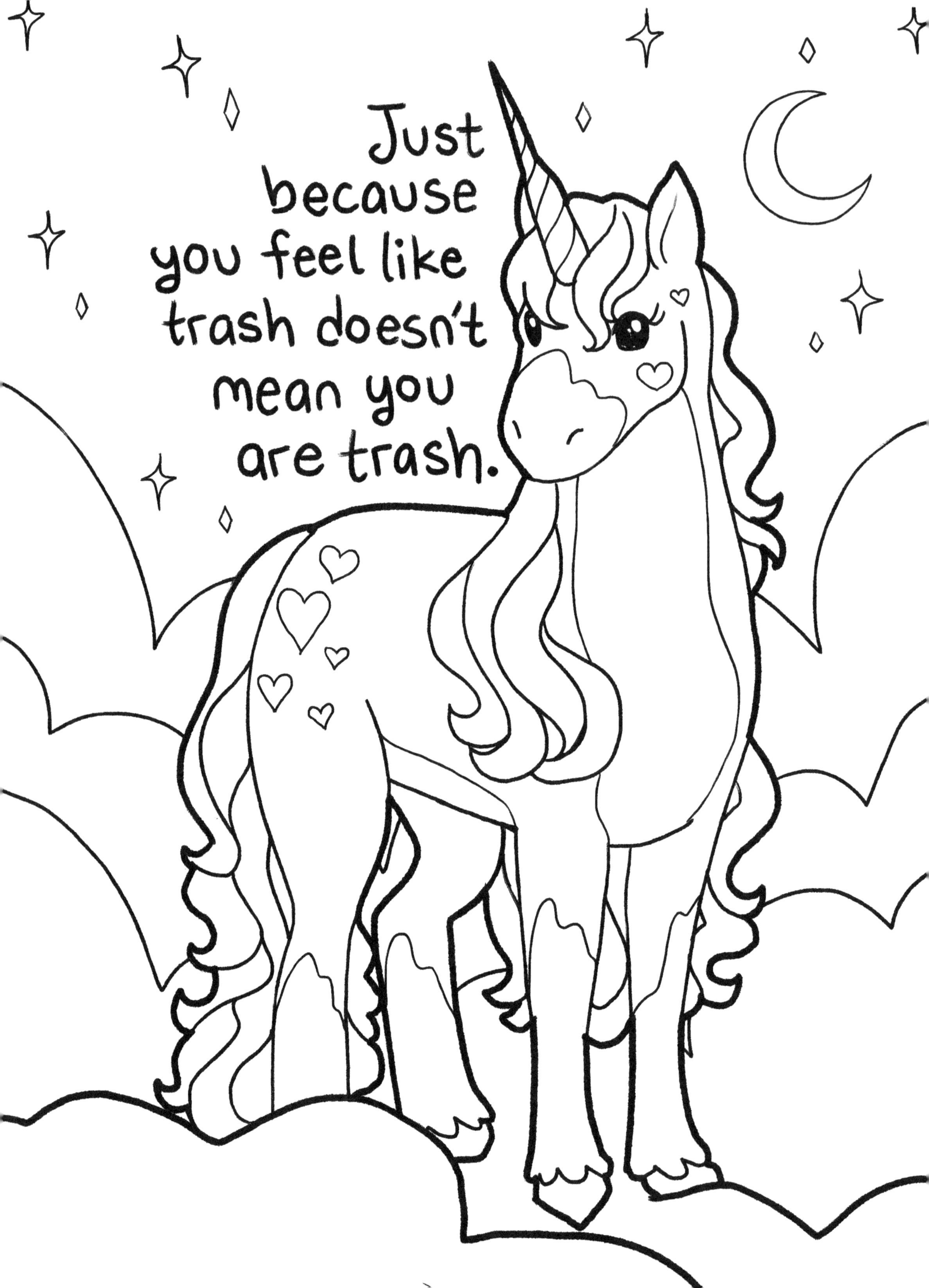
Just because you feel like trash doesn't mean you are trash.

There's
no rule
that says
you have
to have
everything
figured out
right now.
Every step
forward is
progress.

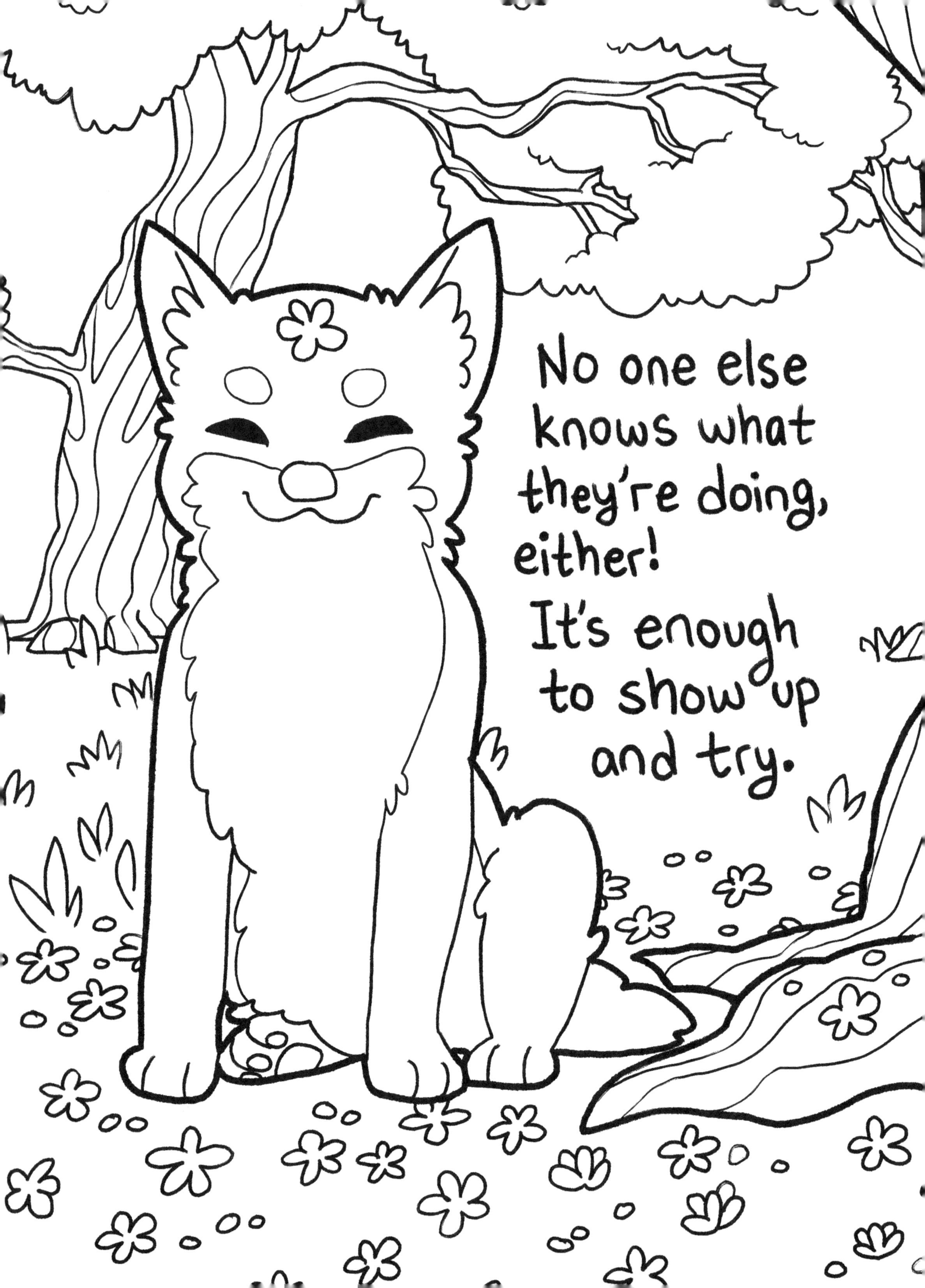

No one else knows what they're doing, either!
It's enough to show up and try.

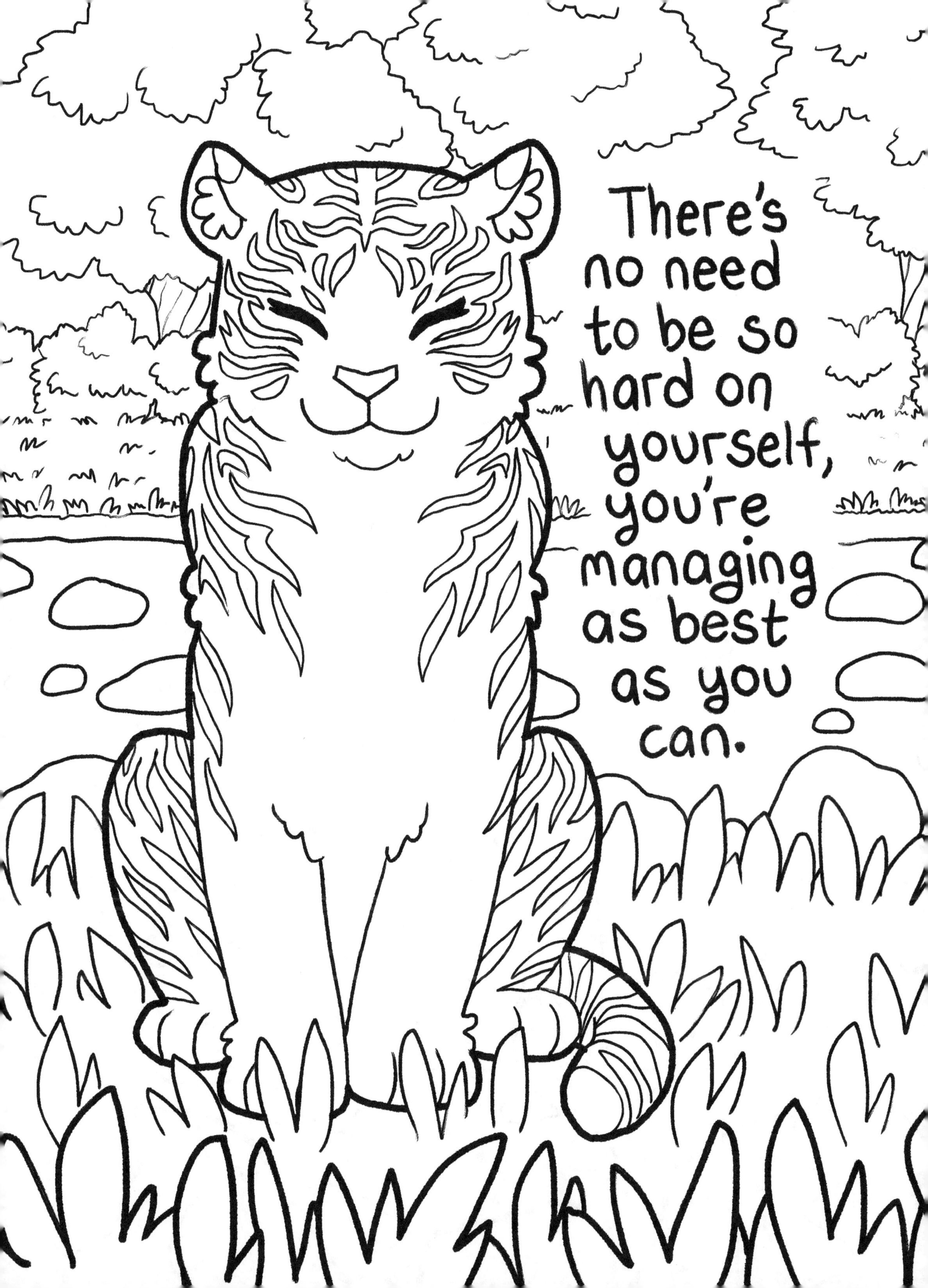
There's no need to be so hard on yourself, you're managing as best as you can.

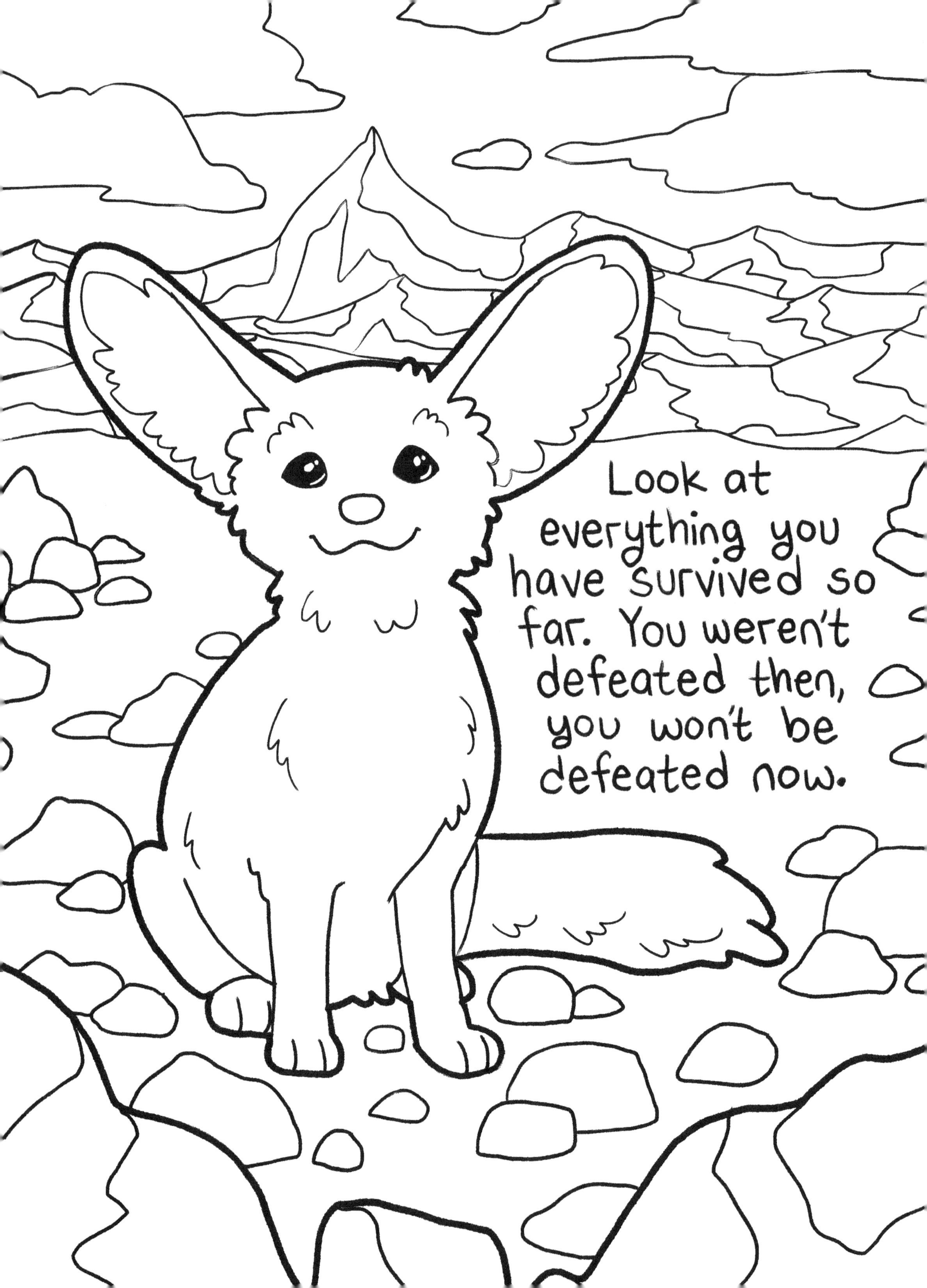
Look at everything you have survived so far. You weren't defeated then, you won't be defeated now.

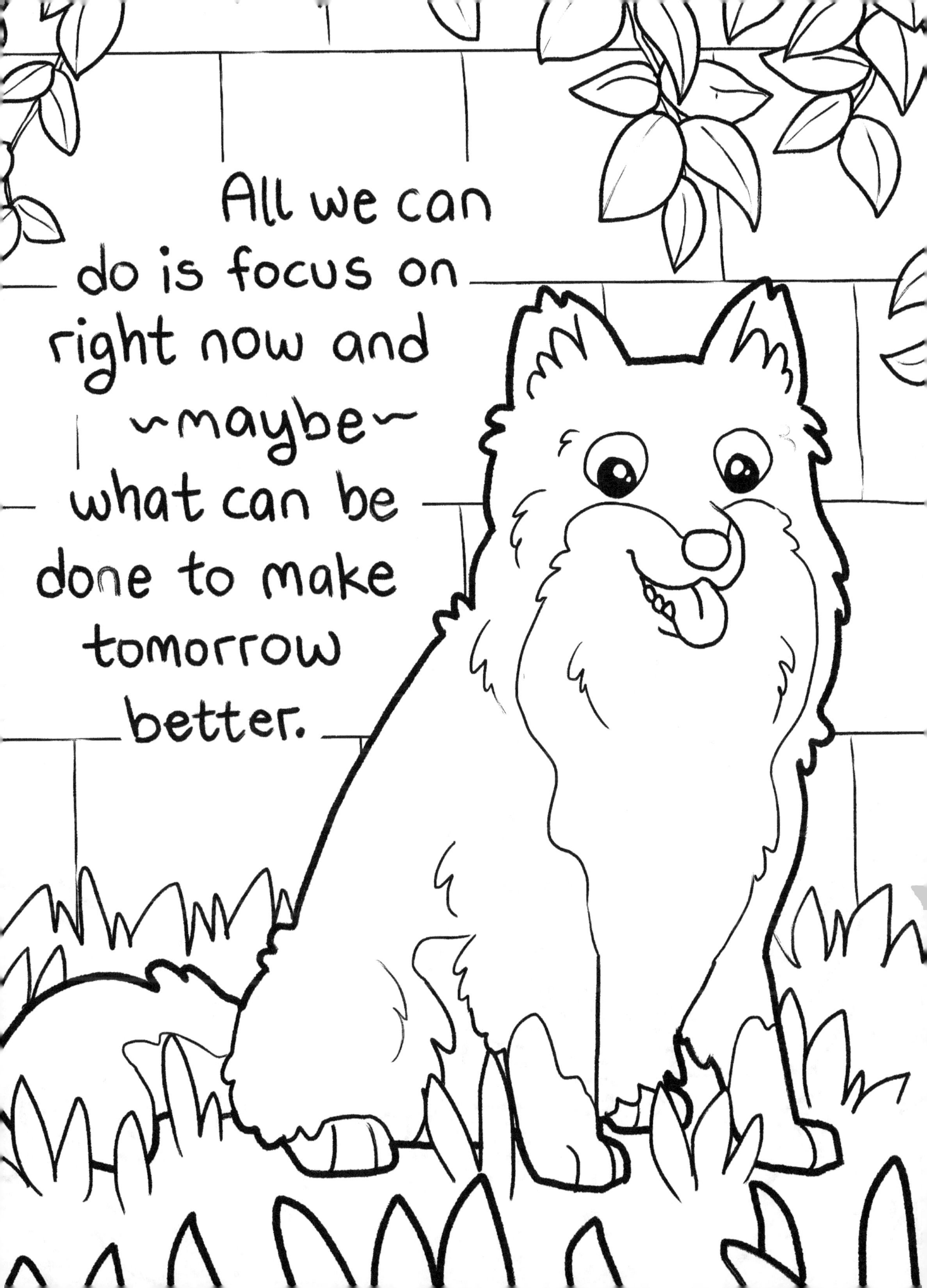

All we can do is focus on right now and ~maybe~ what can be done to make tomorrow better.

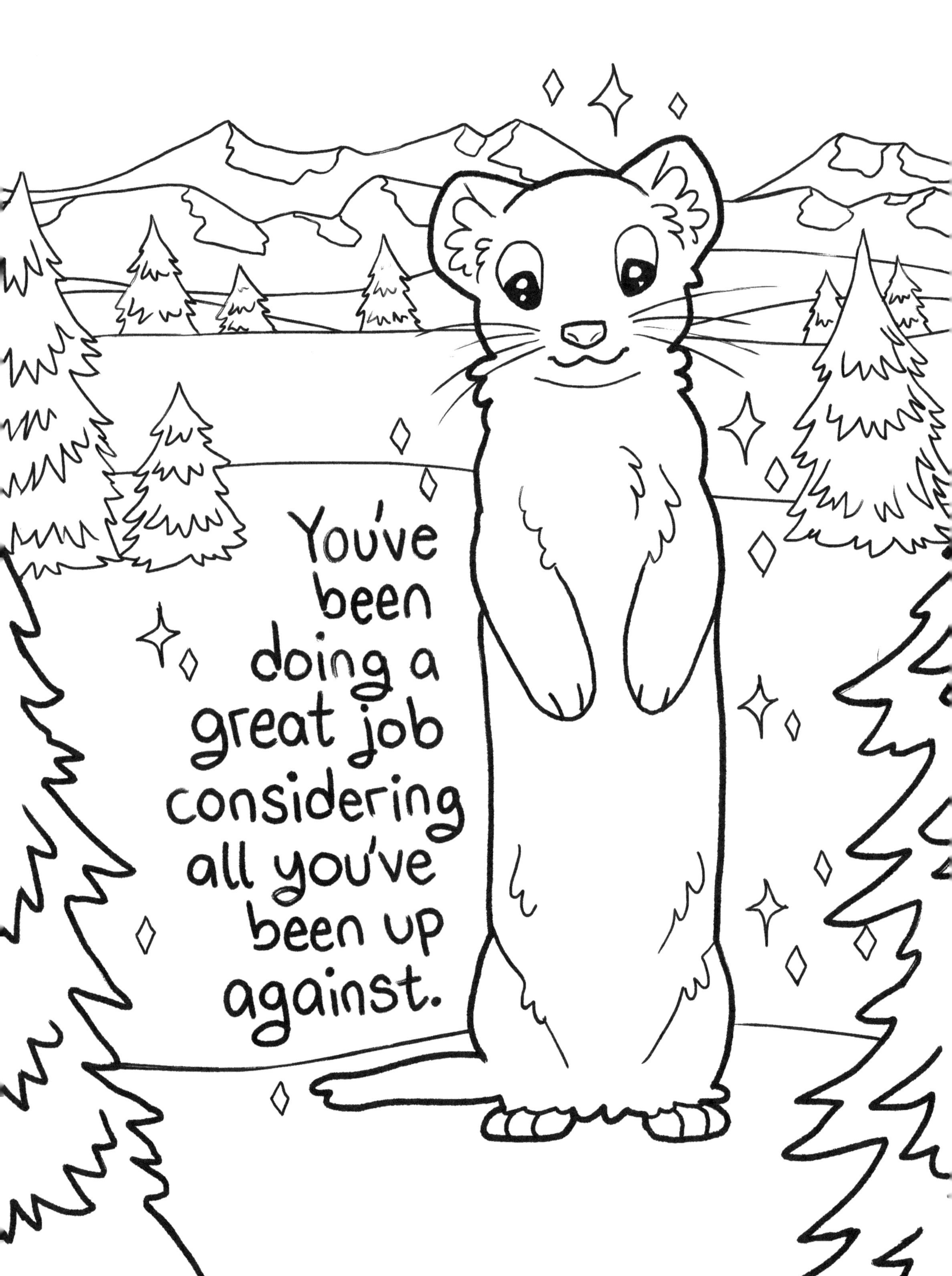
You've been doing a great job considering all you've been up against.

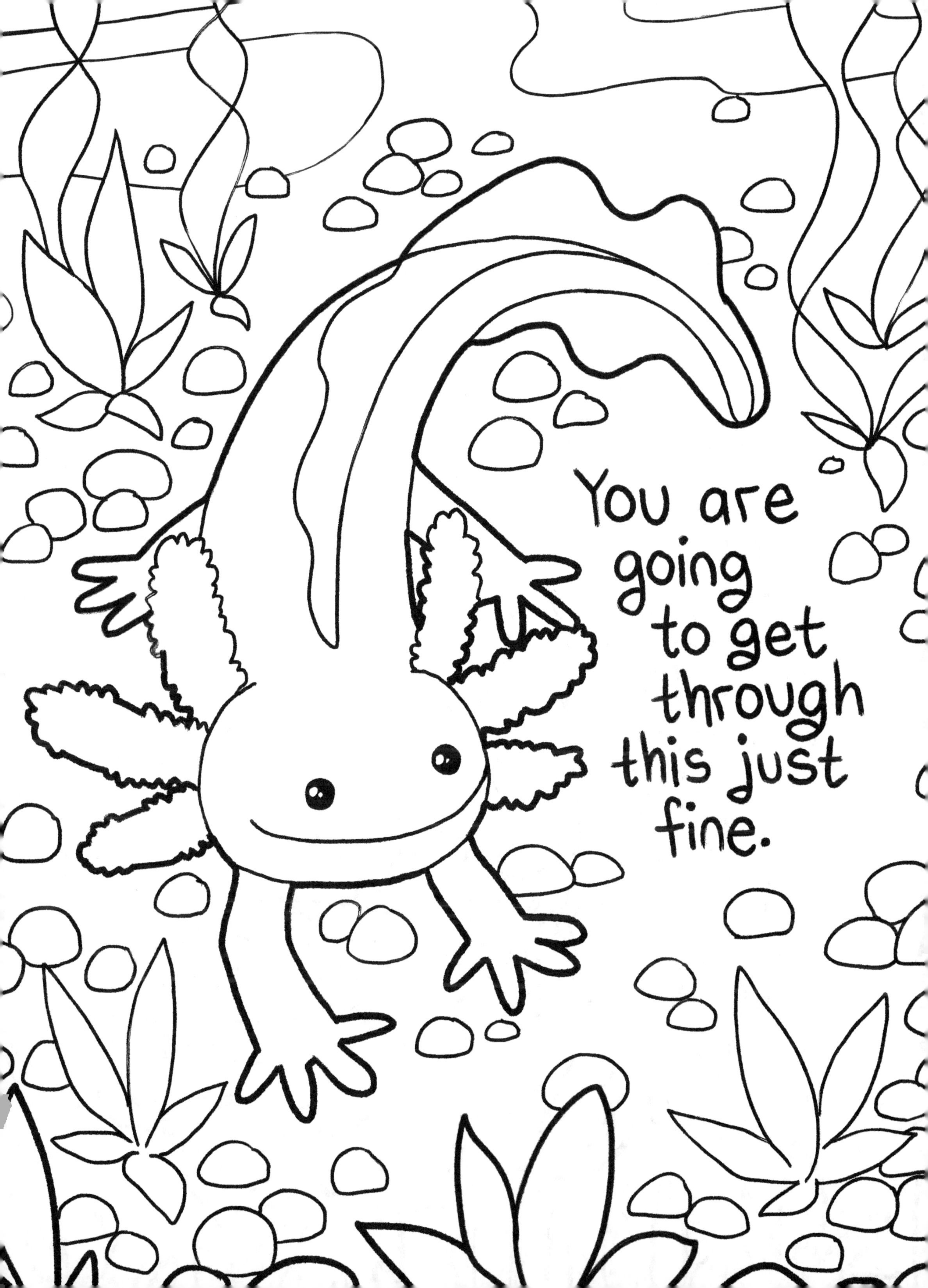
You are going to get through this just fine.

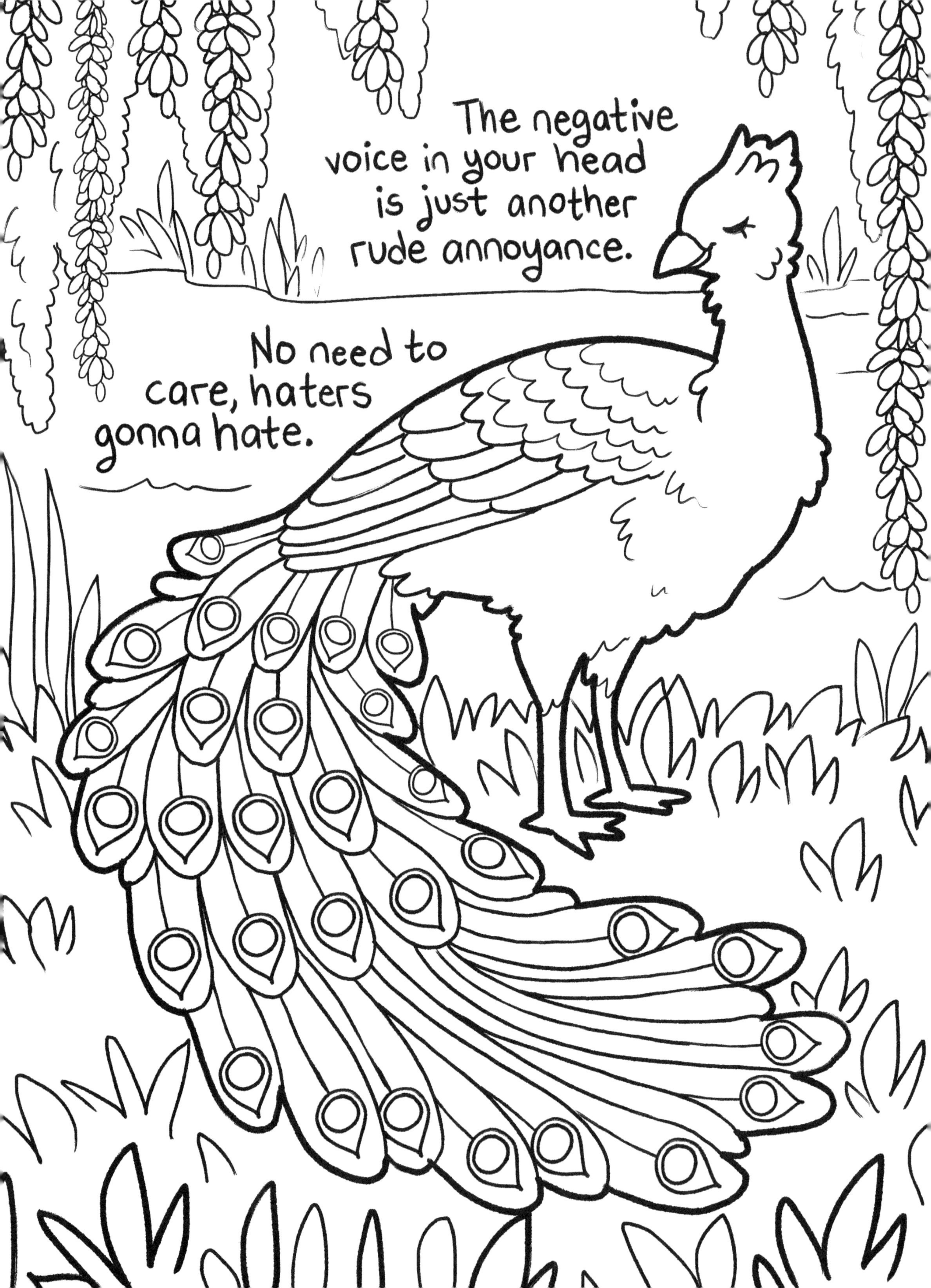
The negative voice in your head is just another rude annoyance.
No need to care, haters gonna hate.

Feeling worried doesn't mean anything bad is going to happen.

You're going to get through this fine; you always find a way.

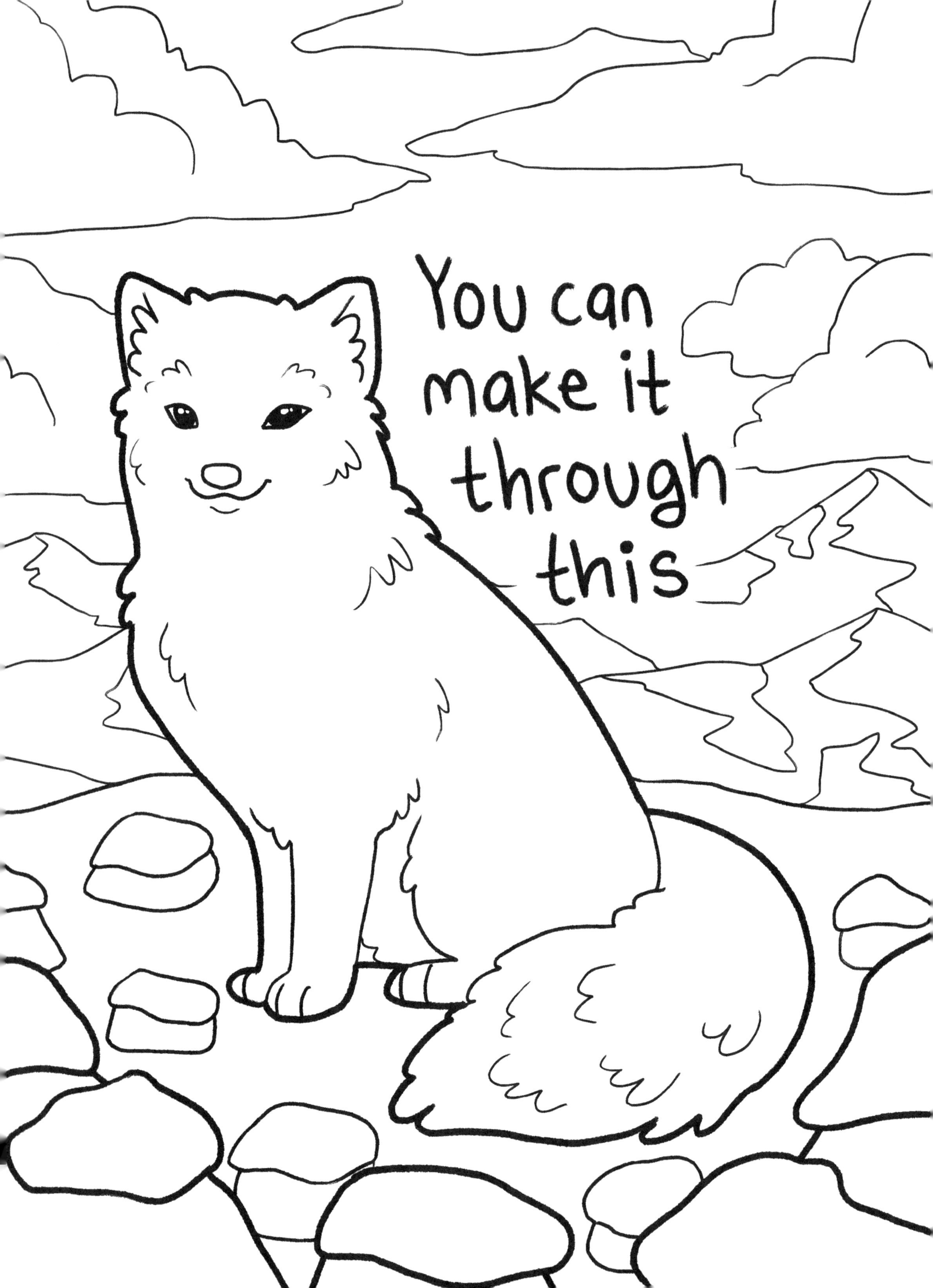
You can
make it
through
this

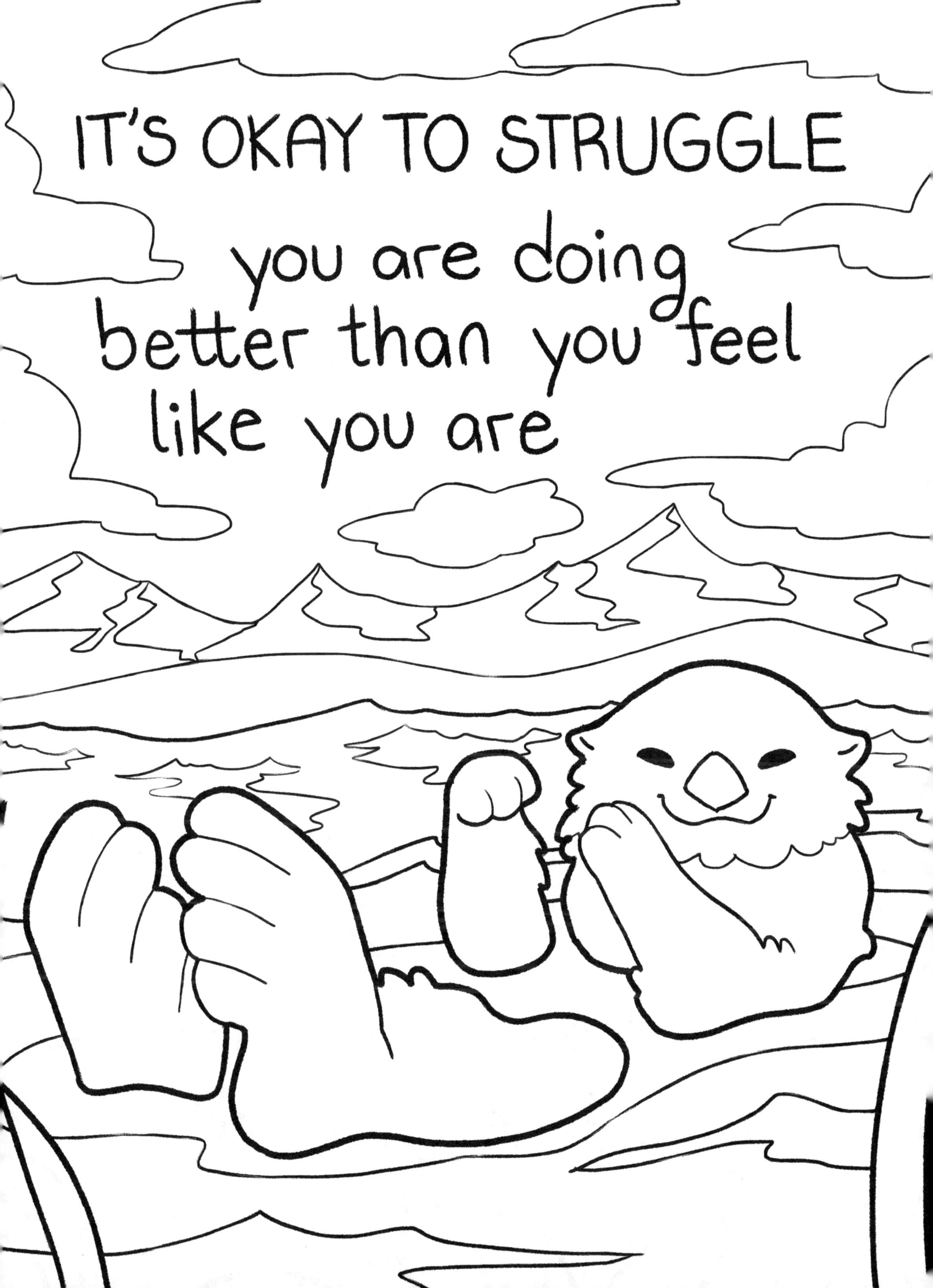
IT'S OKAY TO STRUGGLE
you are doing better than you feel like you are

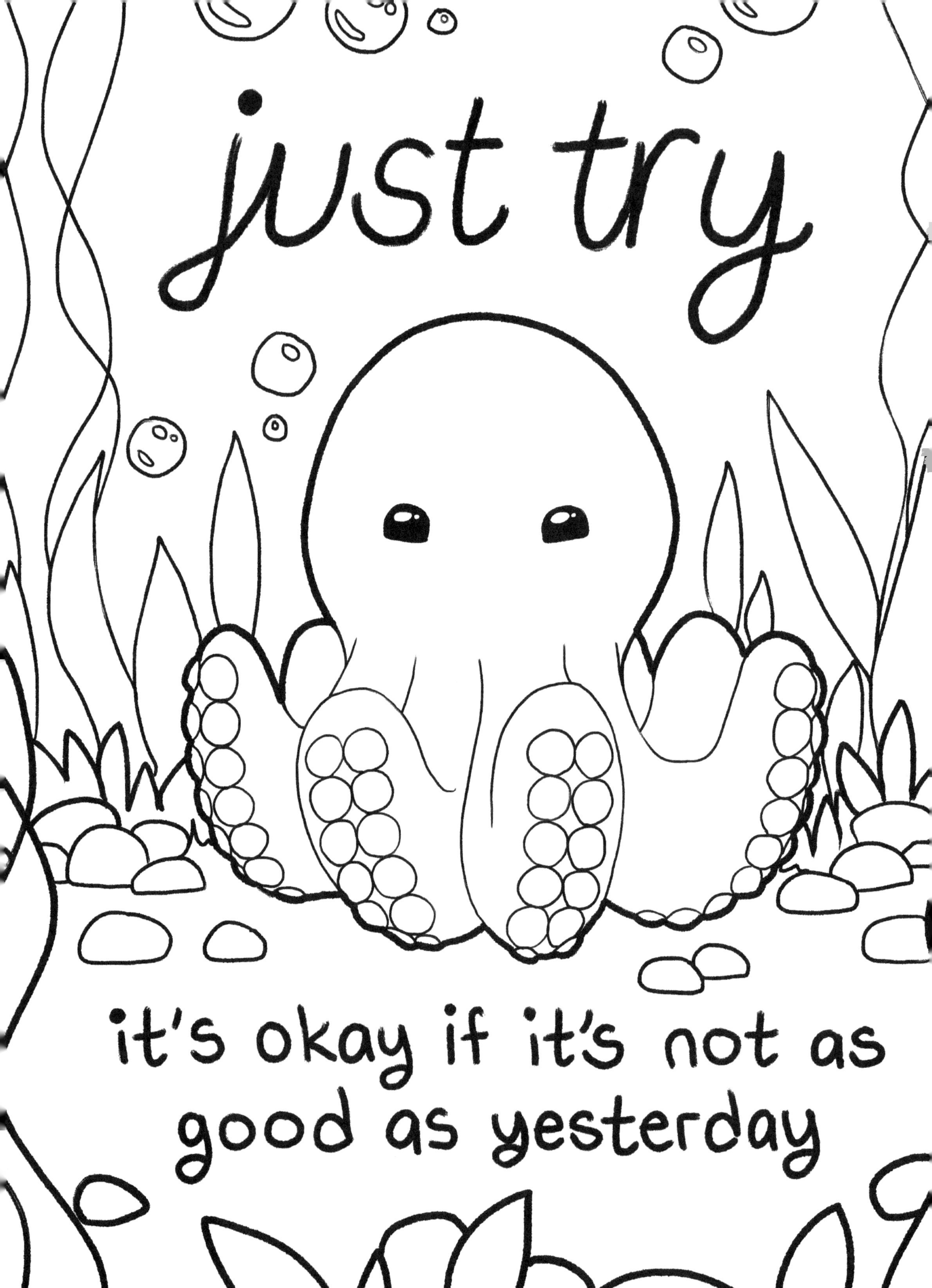
just try
it's okay if it's not as
good as yesterday

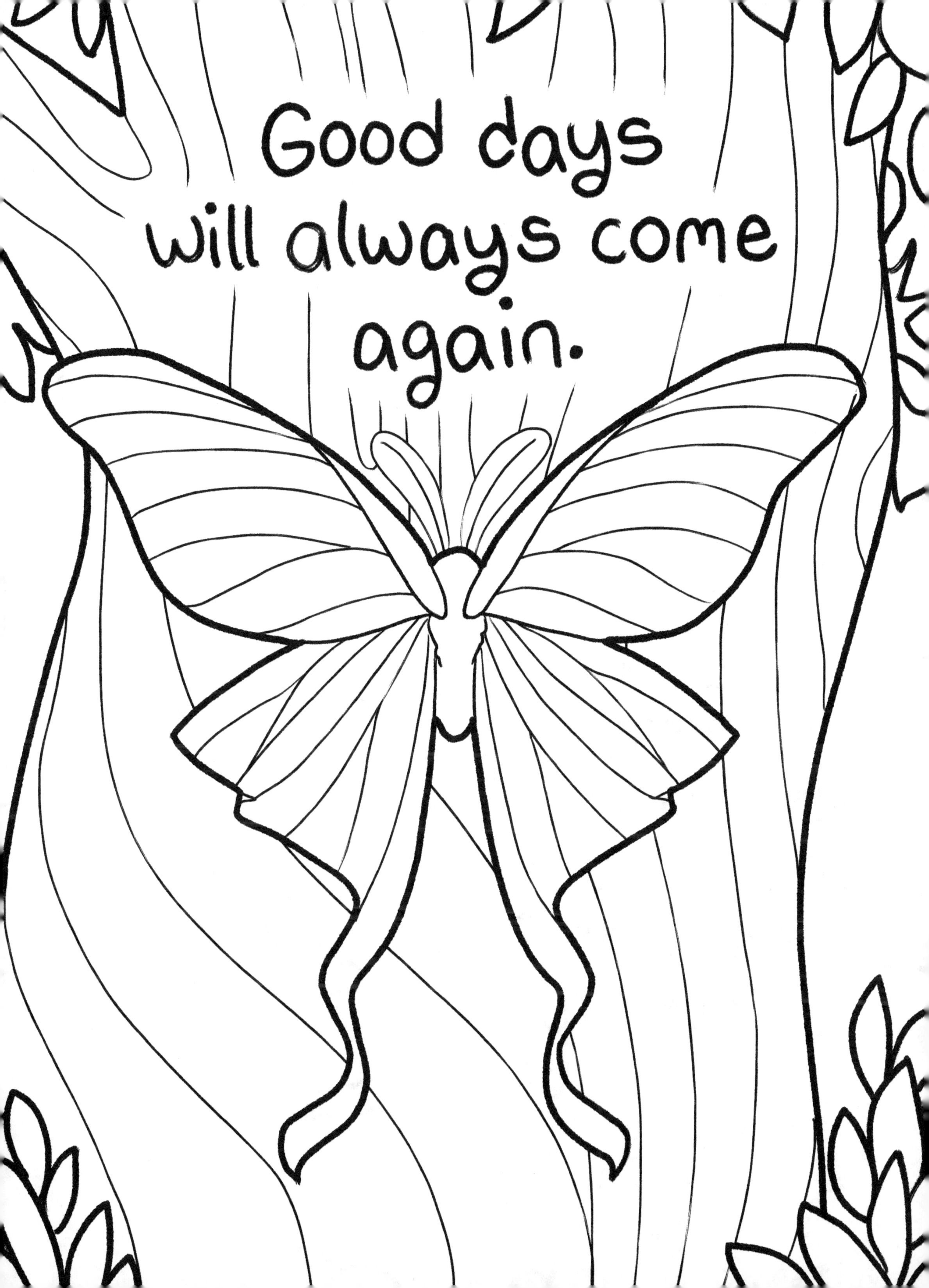
Good days
will always come
again.

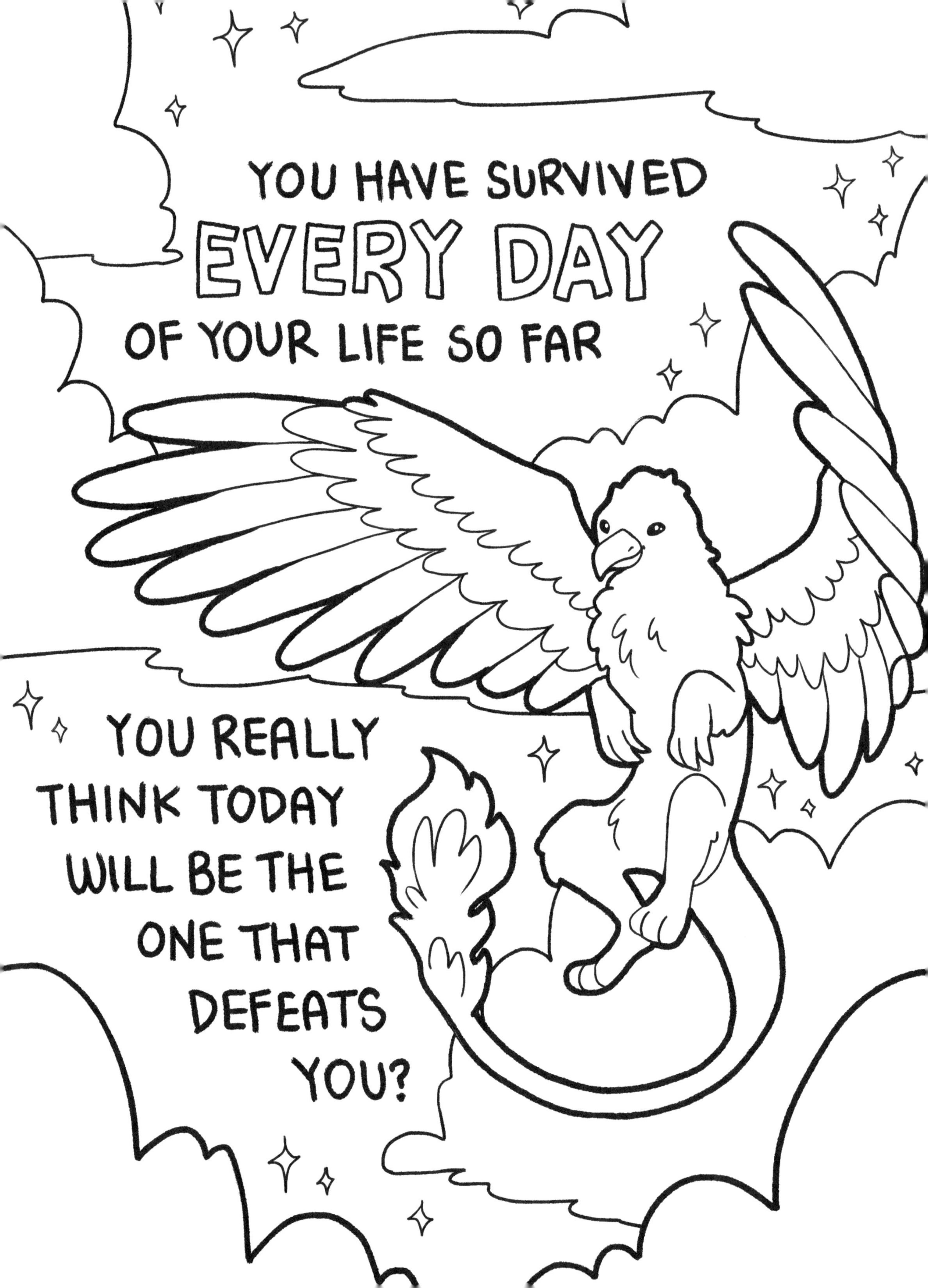
YOU HAVE SURVIVED
EVERY DAY
OF YOUR LIFE SO FAR
YOU REALLY THINK TODAY WILL BE THE ONE THAT DEFEATS YOU?

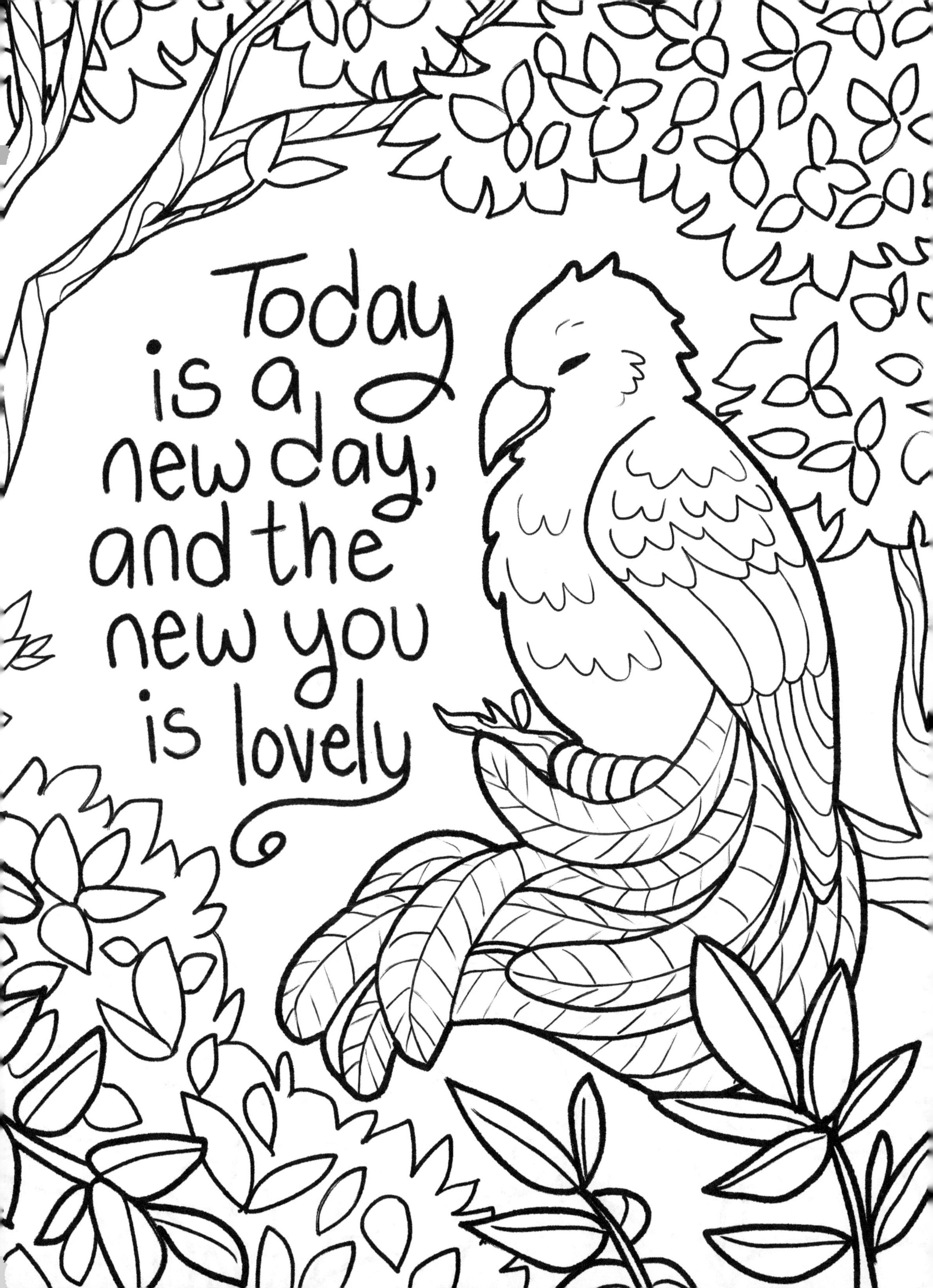
Today
is a
new day,
and the
new you
is lovely

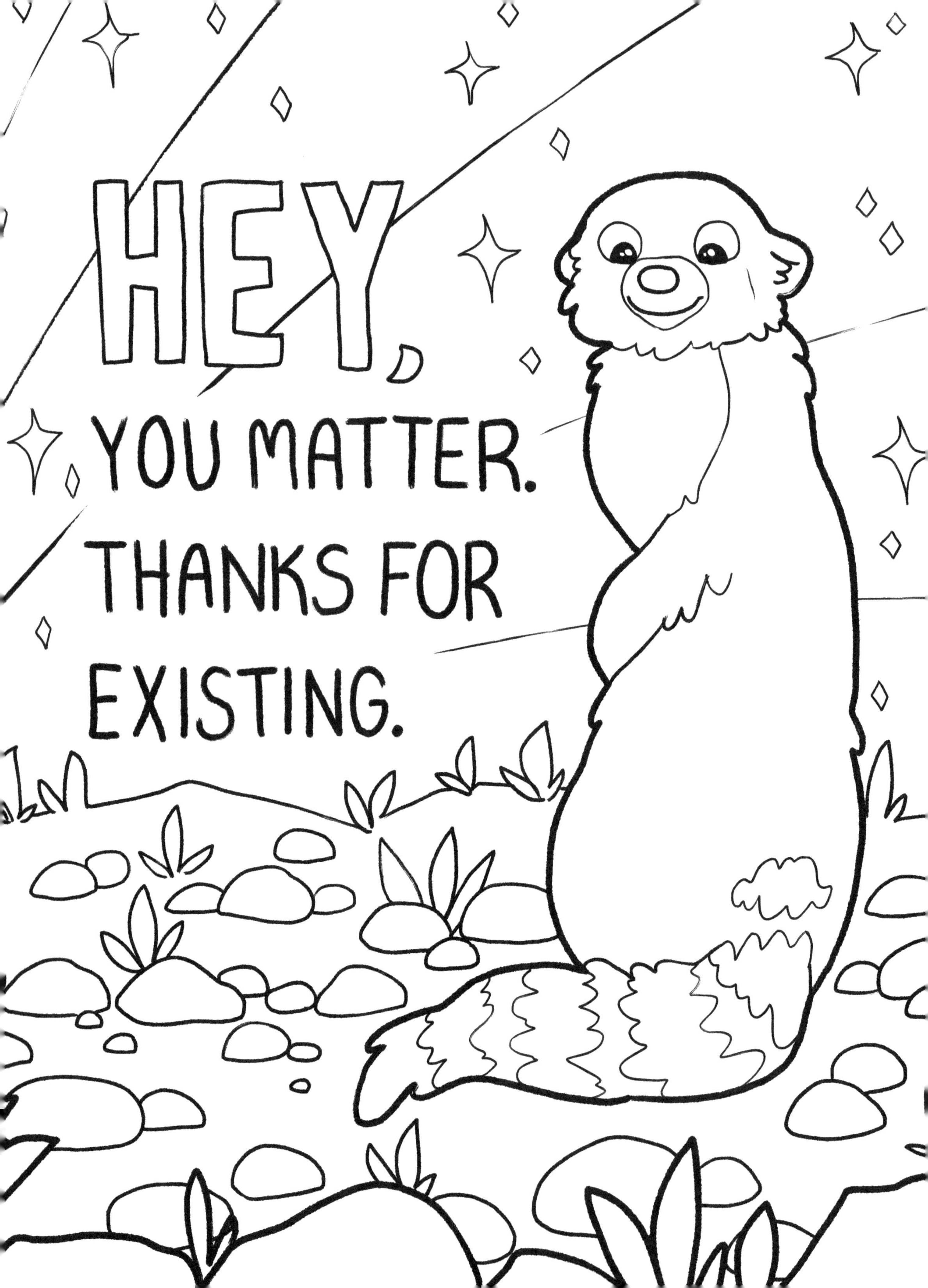
HEY,
YOU MATTER.
THANKS FOR
EXISTING.

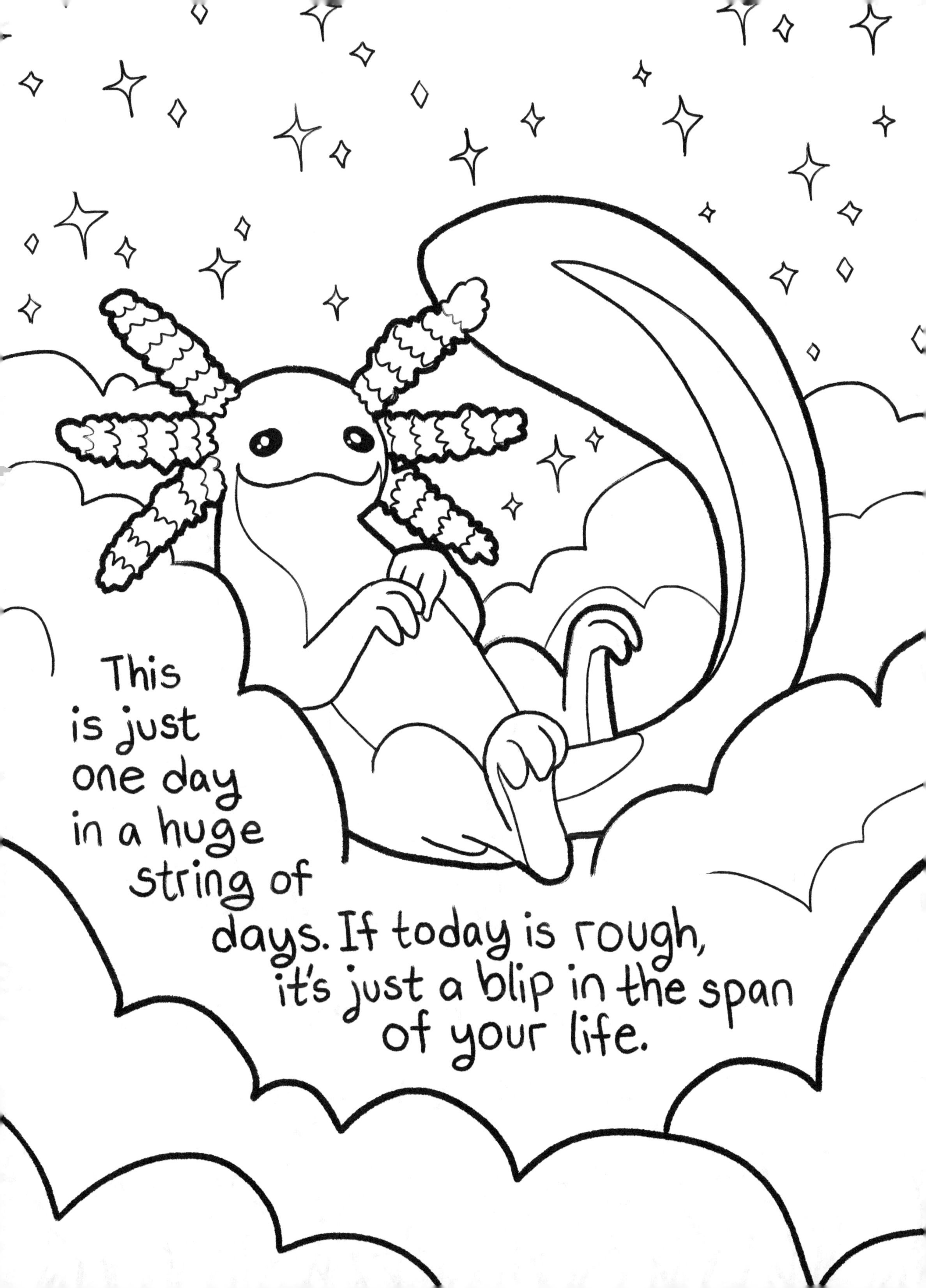
This is just one day in a huge string of days. If today is rough, it's just a blip in the span of your life.

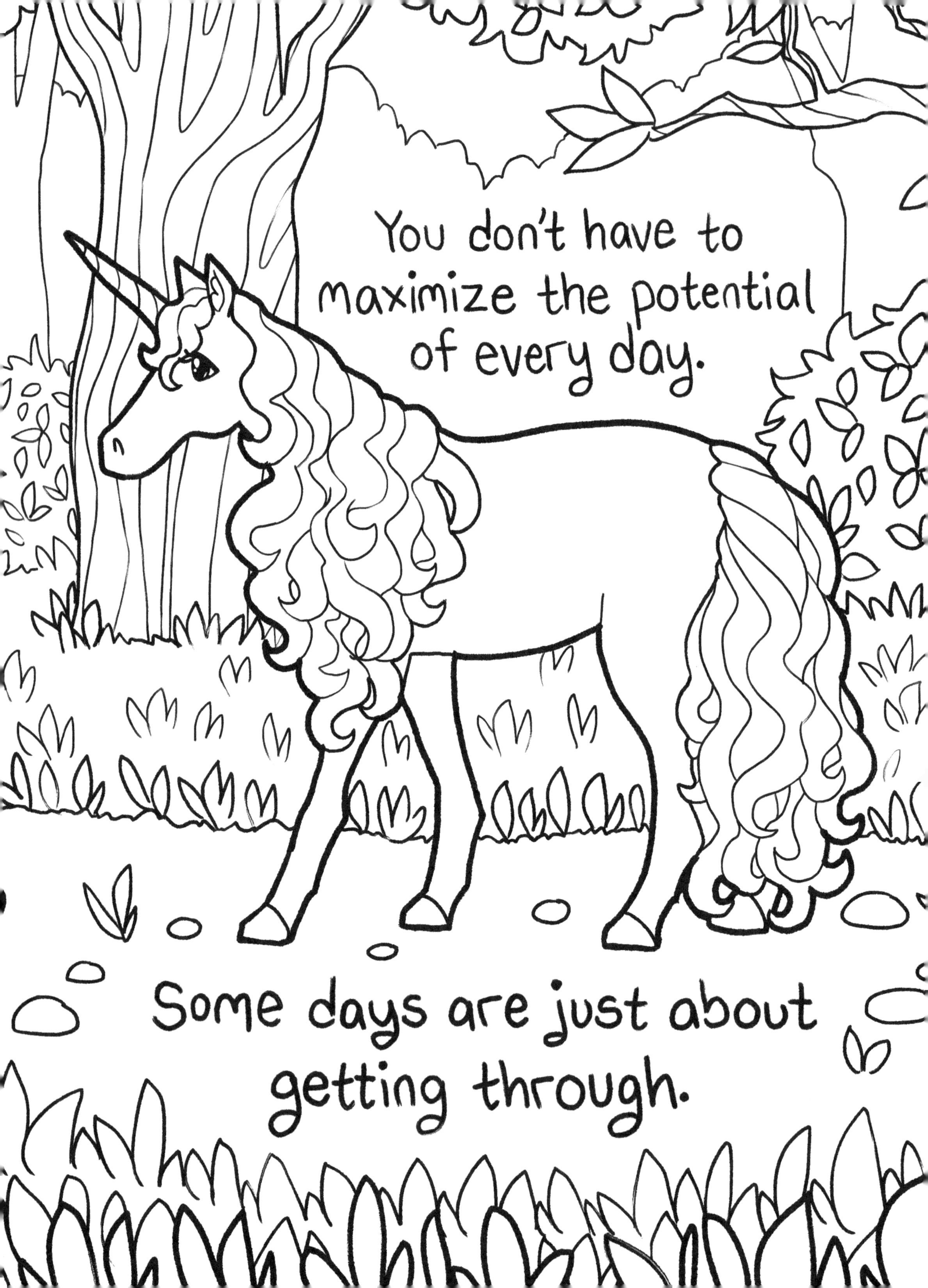
You don't have to maximize the potential of every day.
Some days are just about getting through.

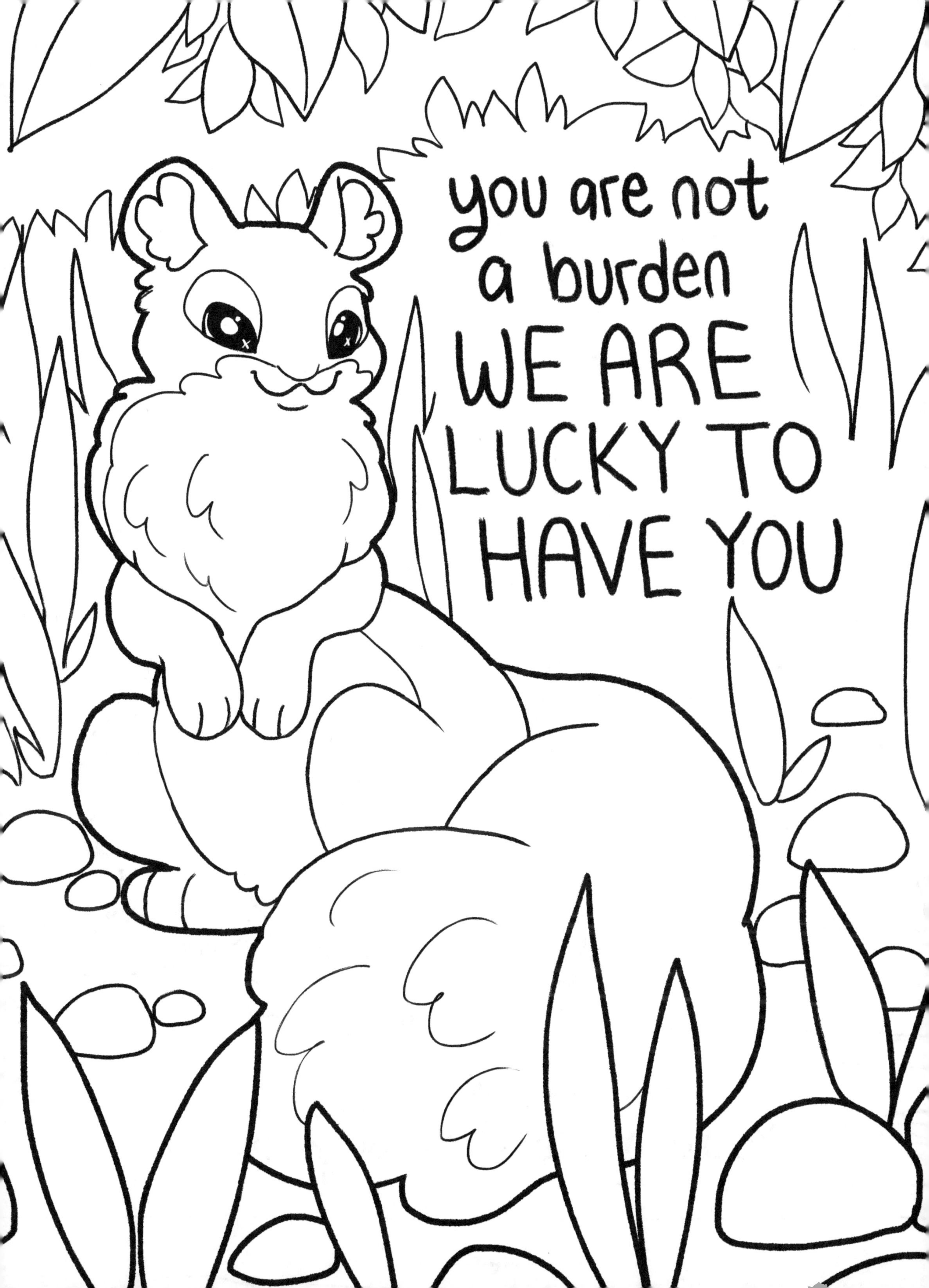
you are not
a burden
WE ARE
LUCKY TO
HAVE YOU

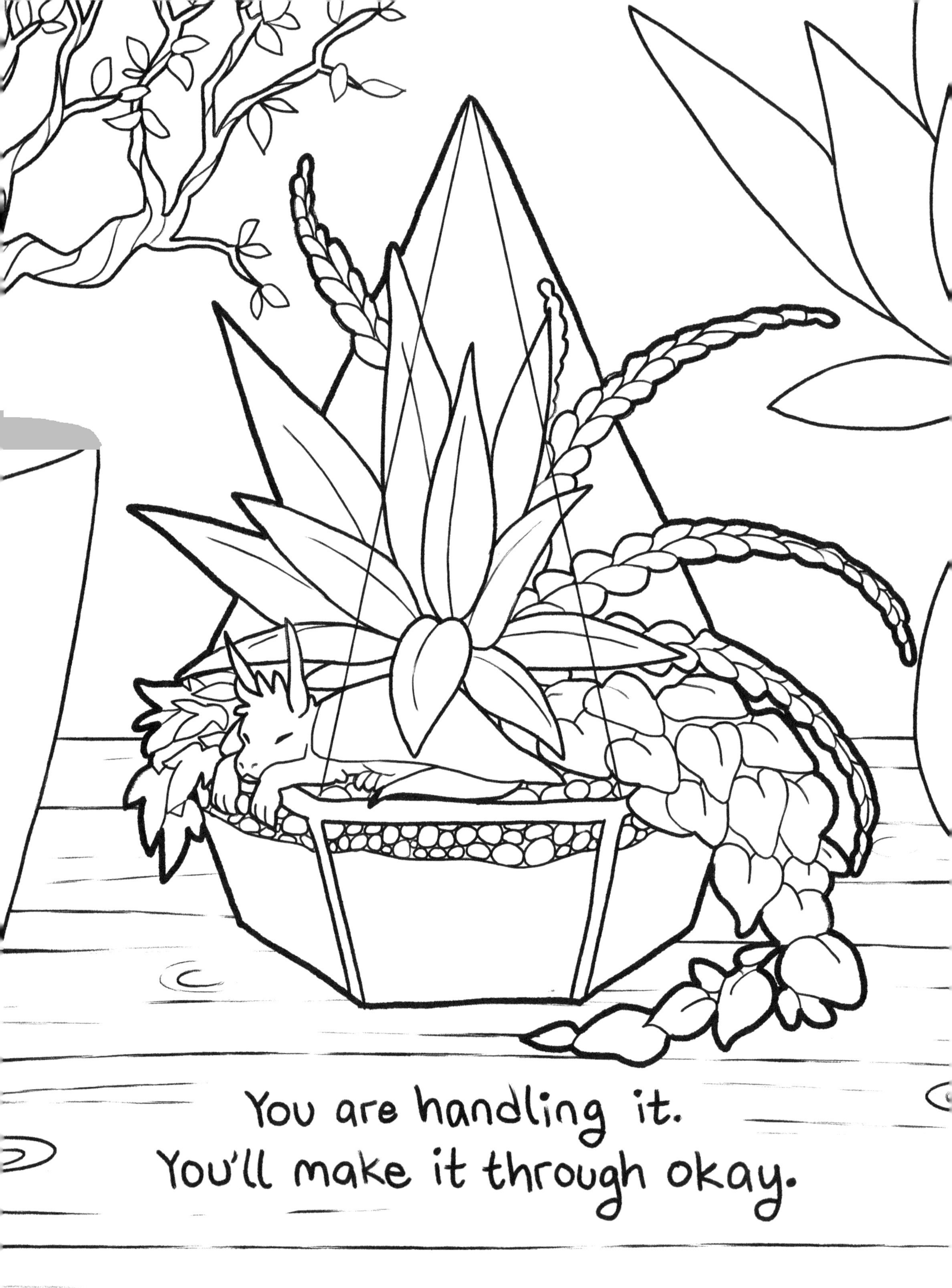
You are handling it.
You'll make it through okay.

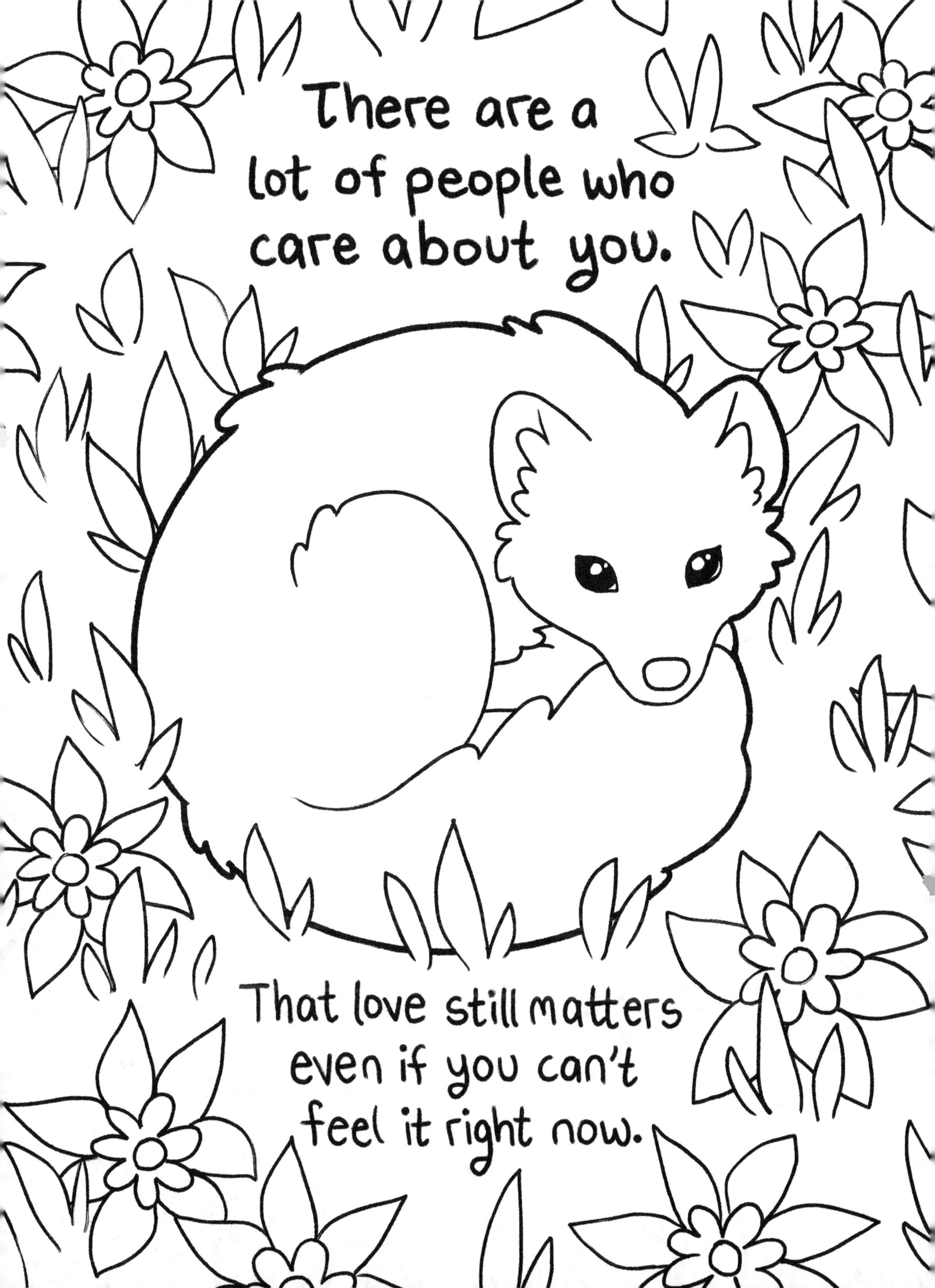
There are a
lot of people who
care about you.
That love still matters
even if you can't
feel it right now.

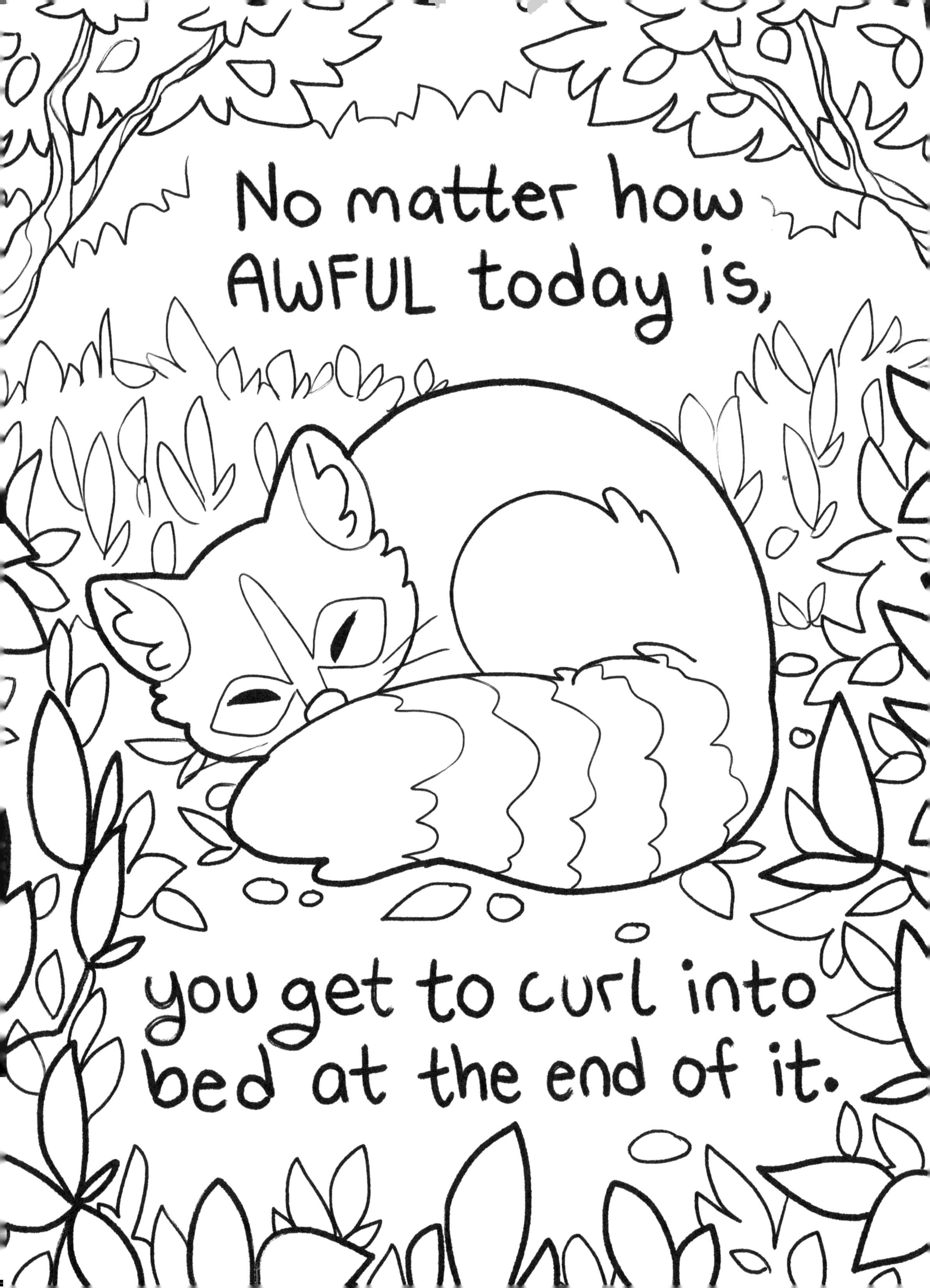

No matter how AWFUL today is,

you get to curl into bed at the end of it.

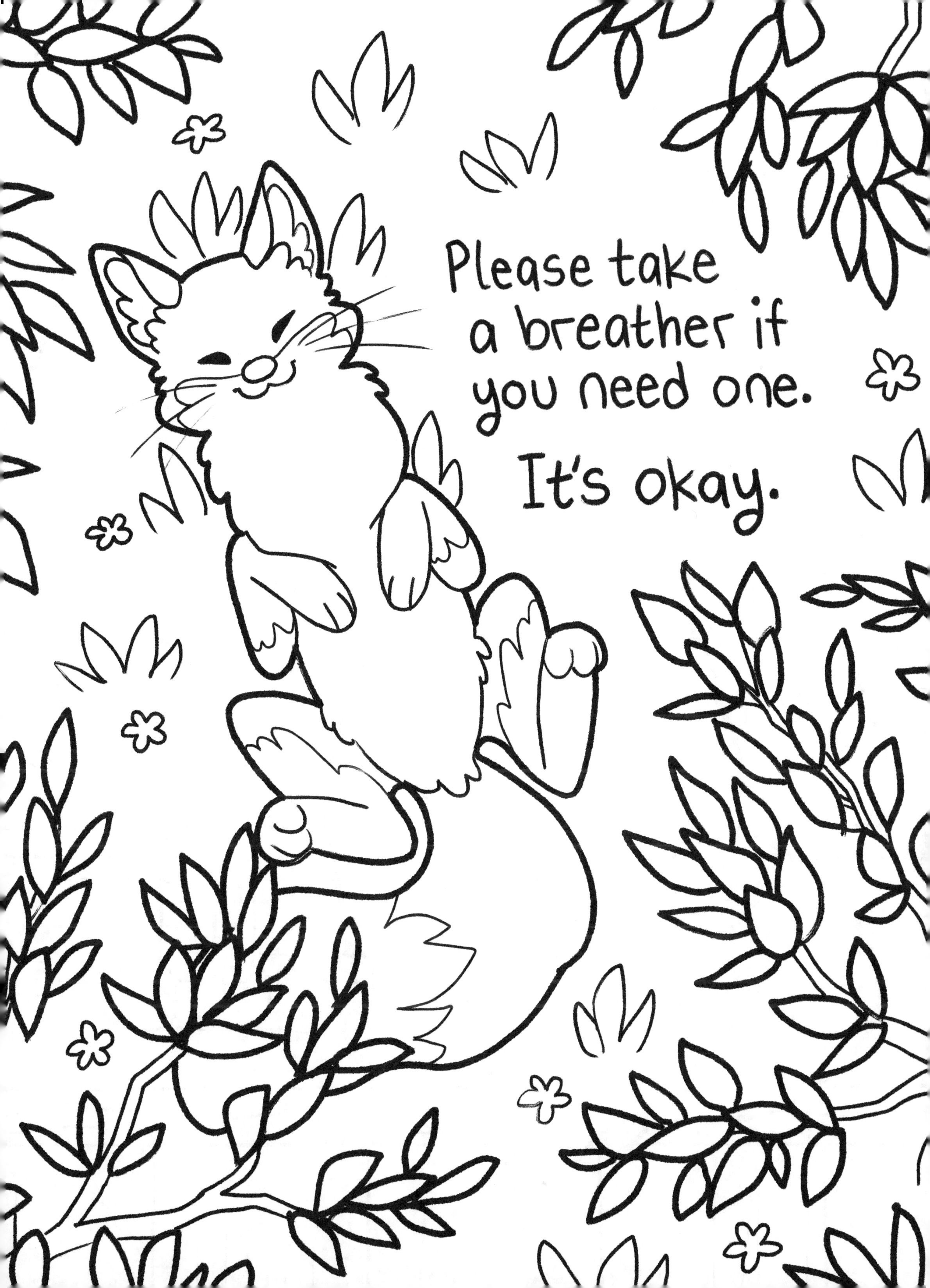
Please take
a breather if
you need one.
It's okay.

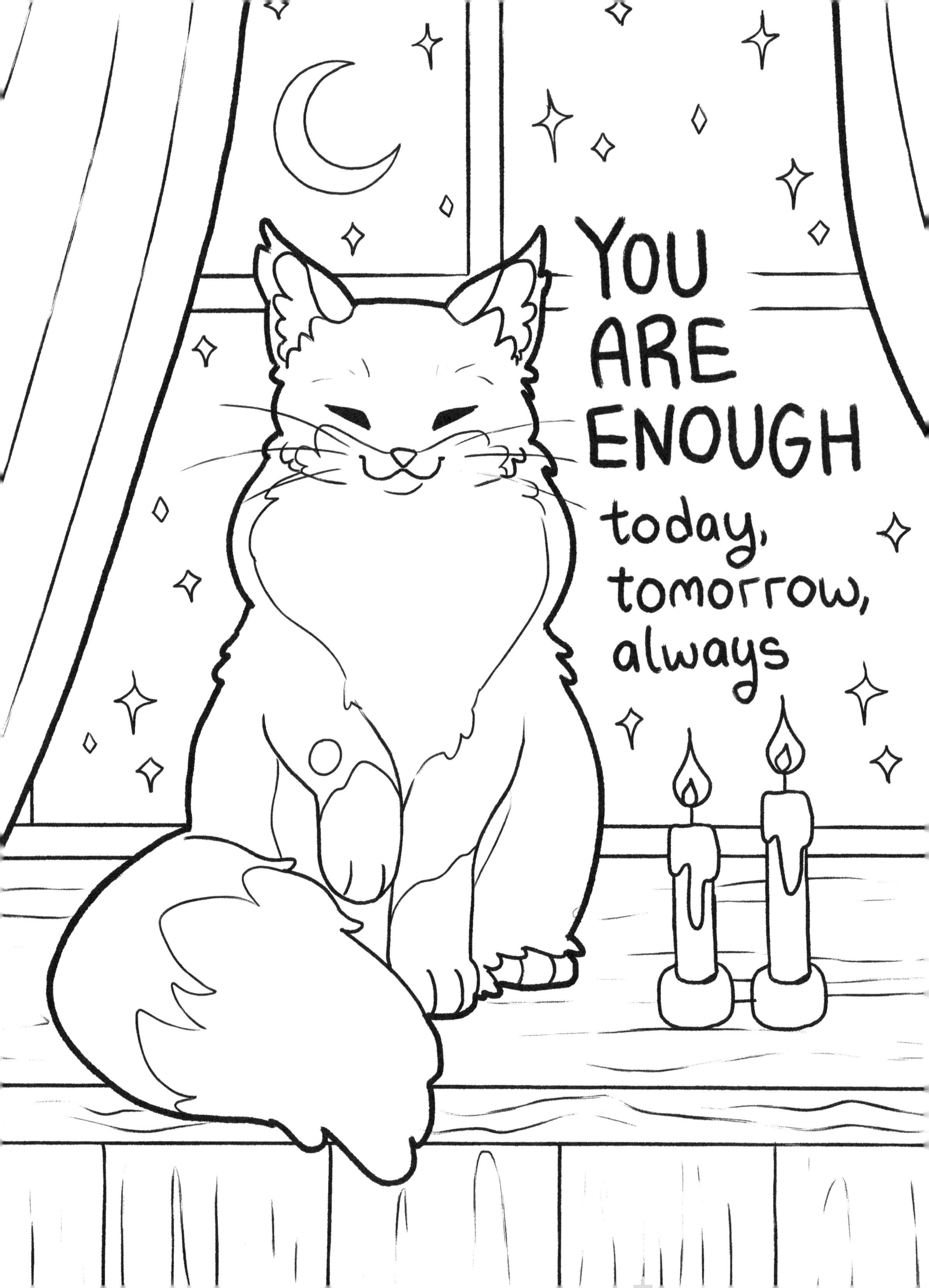
YOU
ARE
ENOUGH
today,
tomorrow,
always

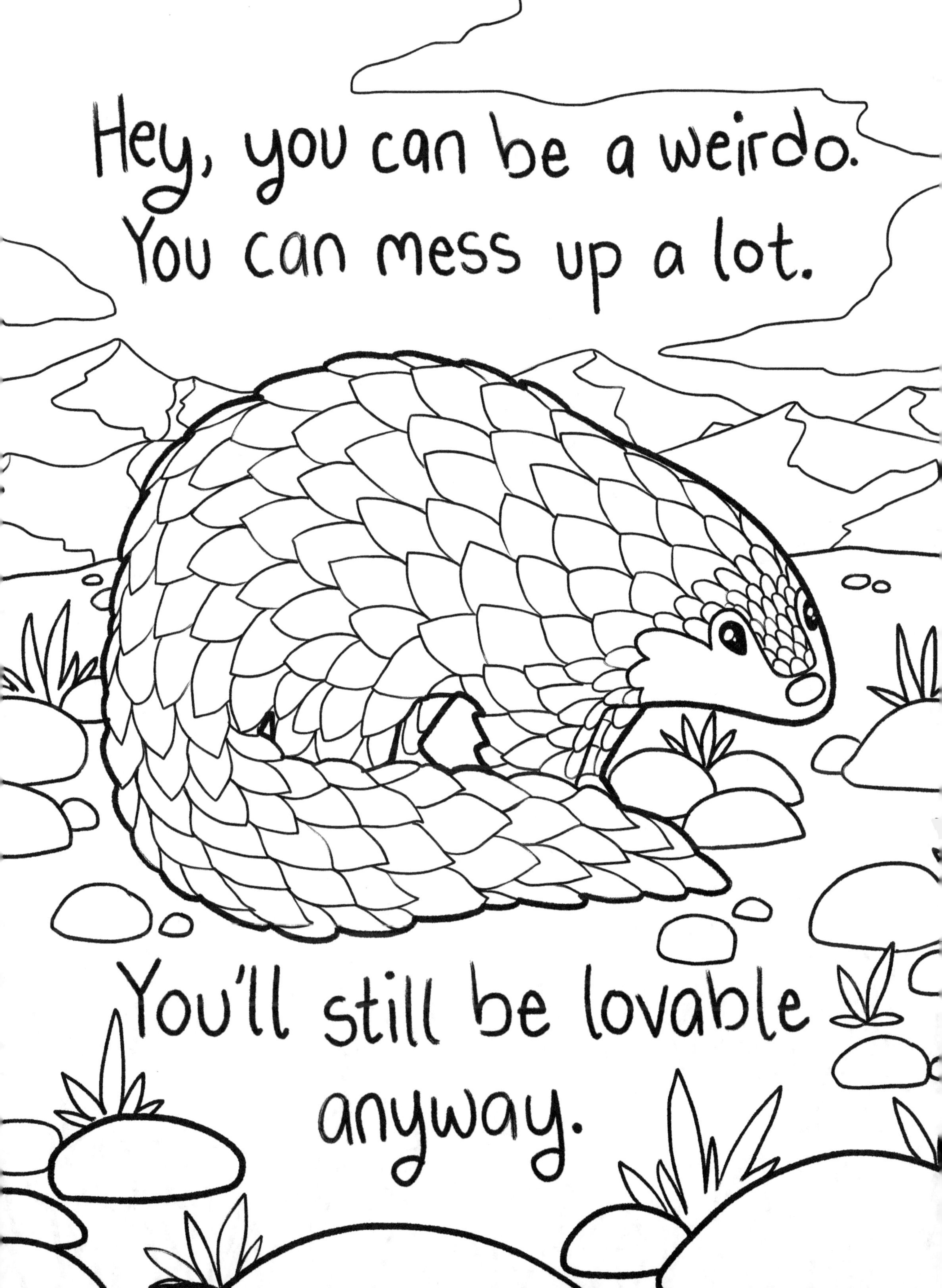
Hey, you can be a weirdo.
You can mess up a lot.
You'll still be lovable
anyway.

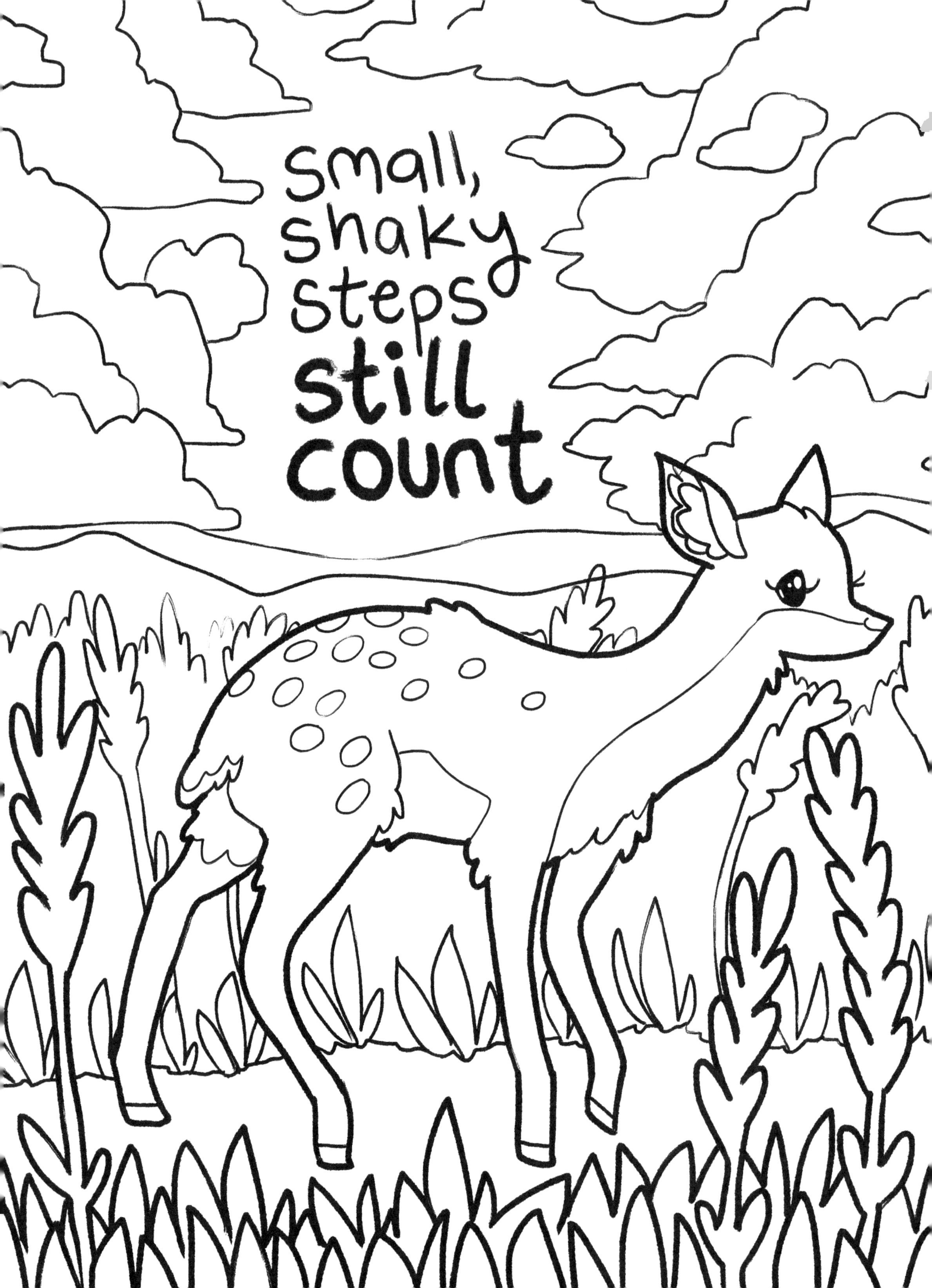
small, shaky steps still count

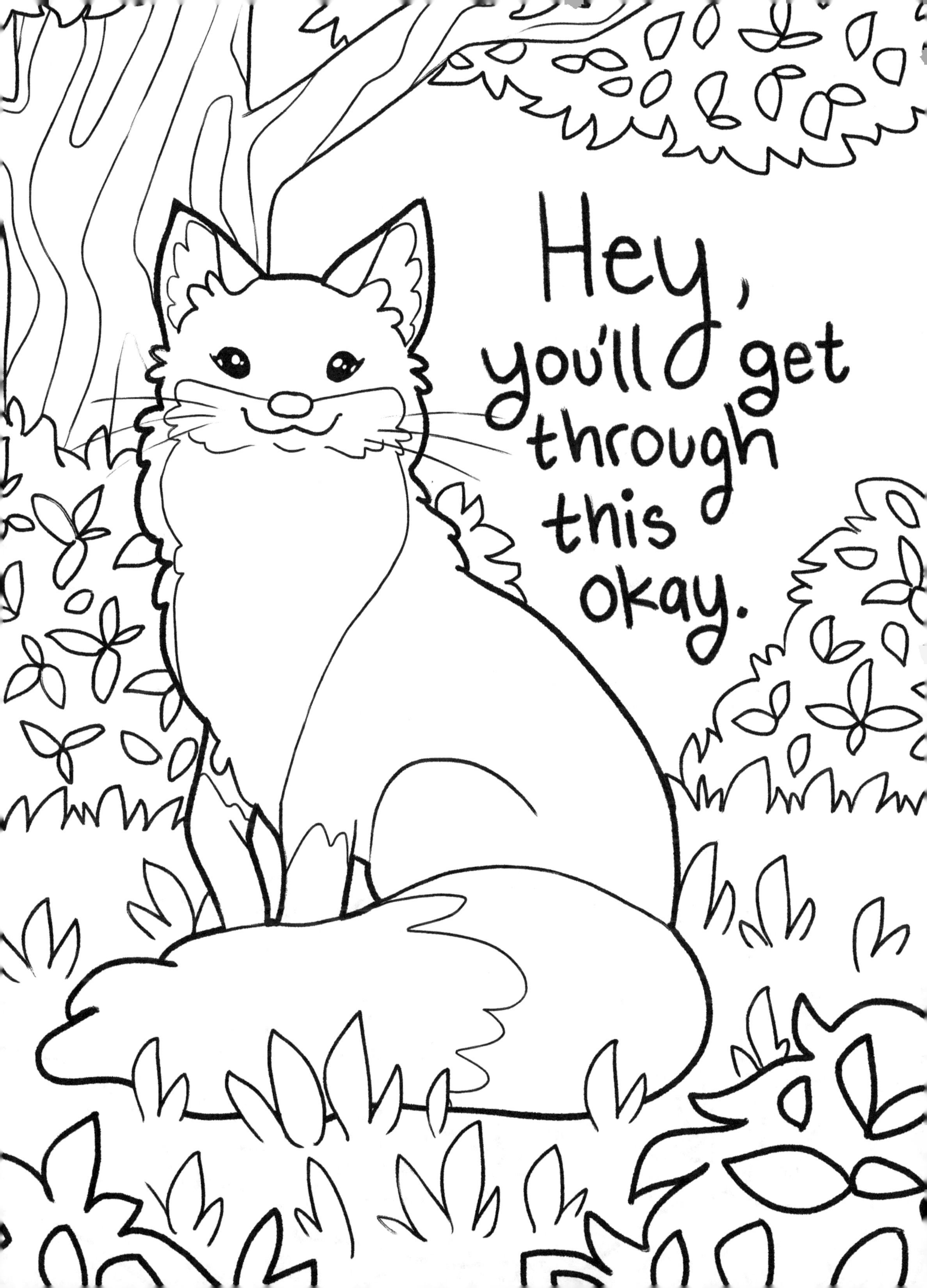

Hey, you'll get through this okay.

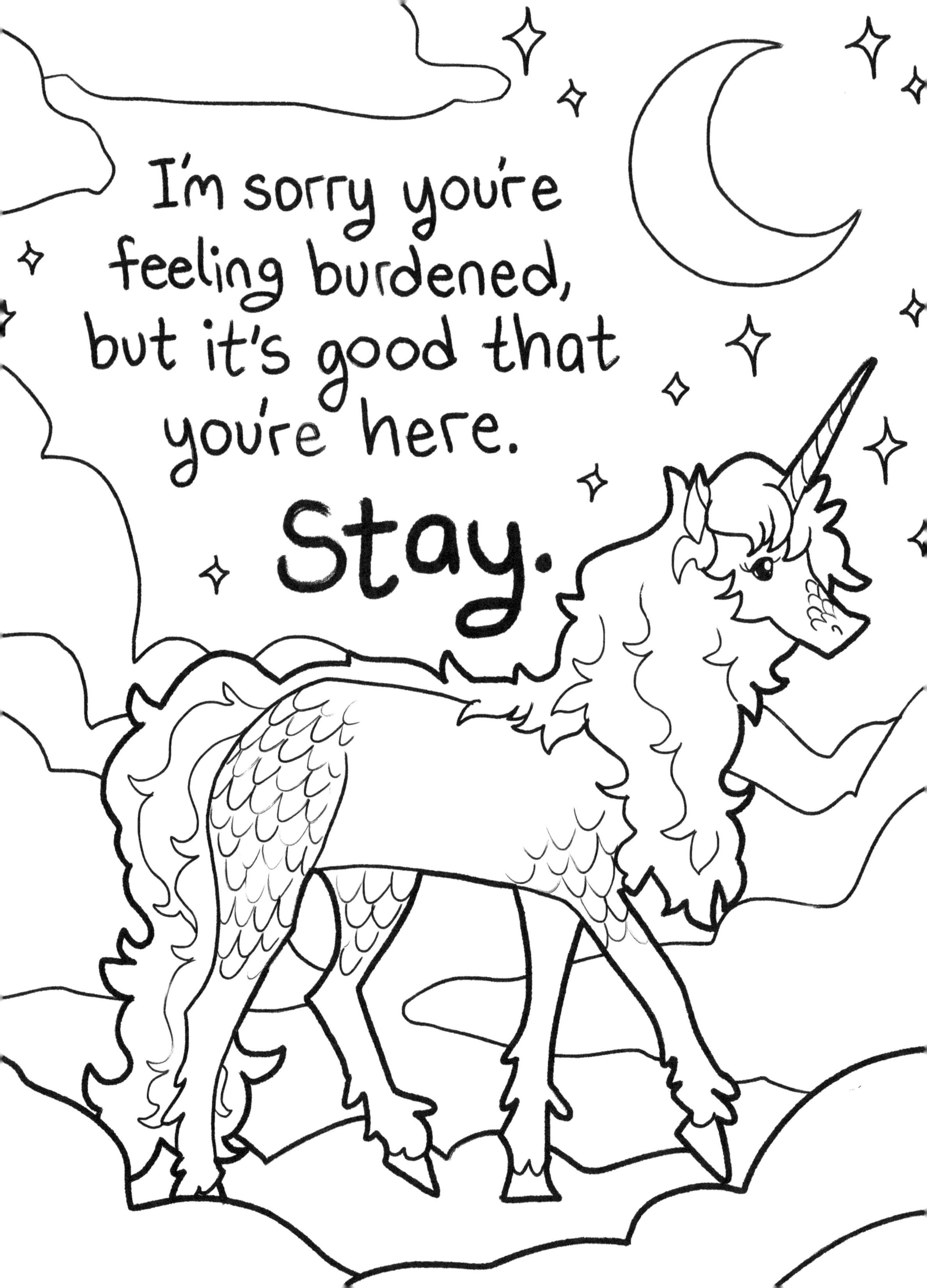
I'm sorry you're feeling burdened, but it's good that you're here.
Stay.

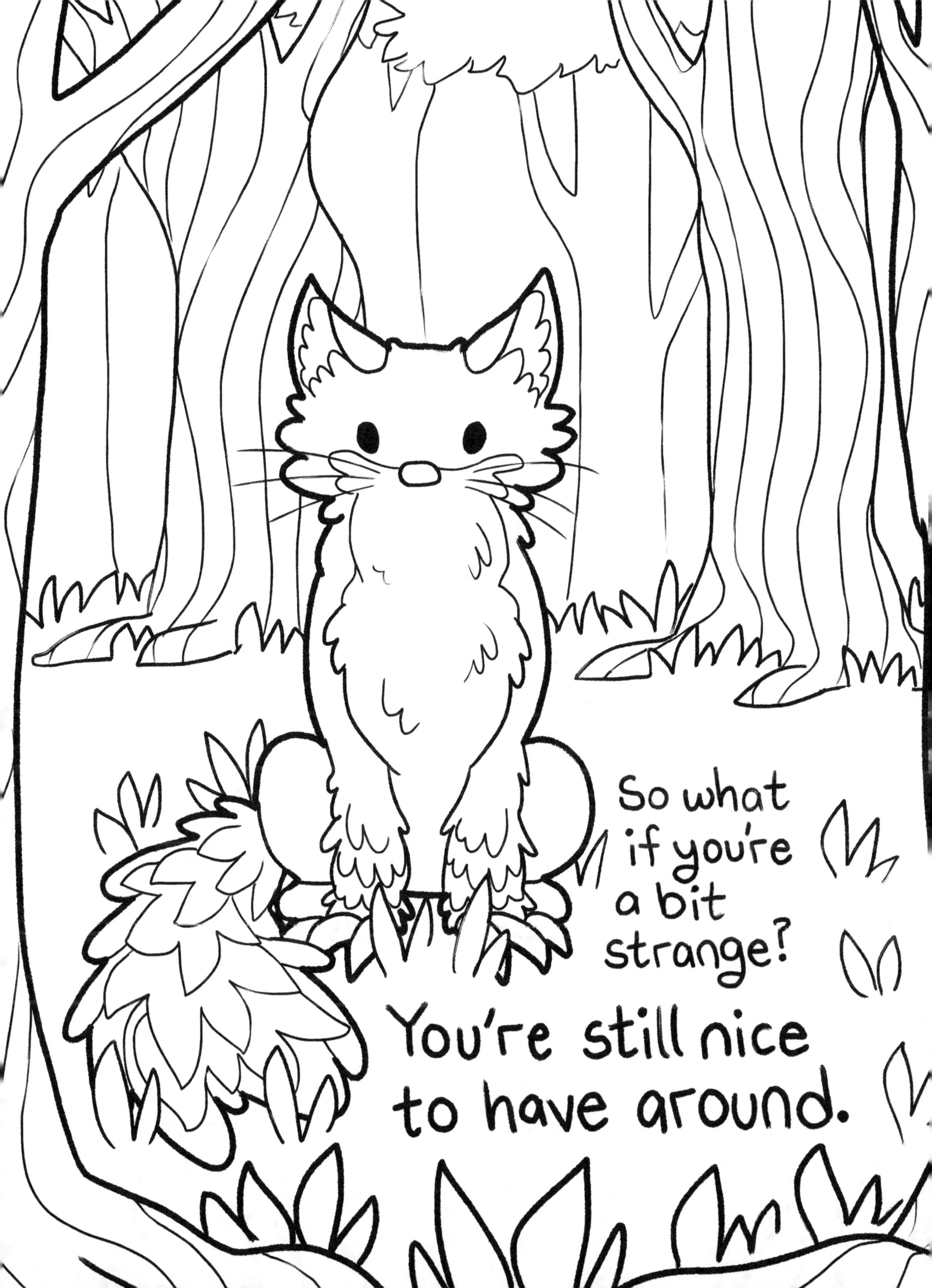
So what if you're a bit strange?
You're still nice to have around.

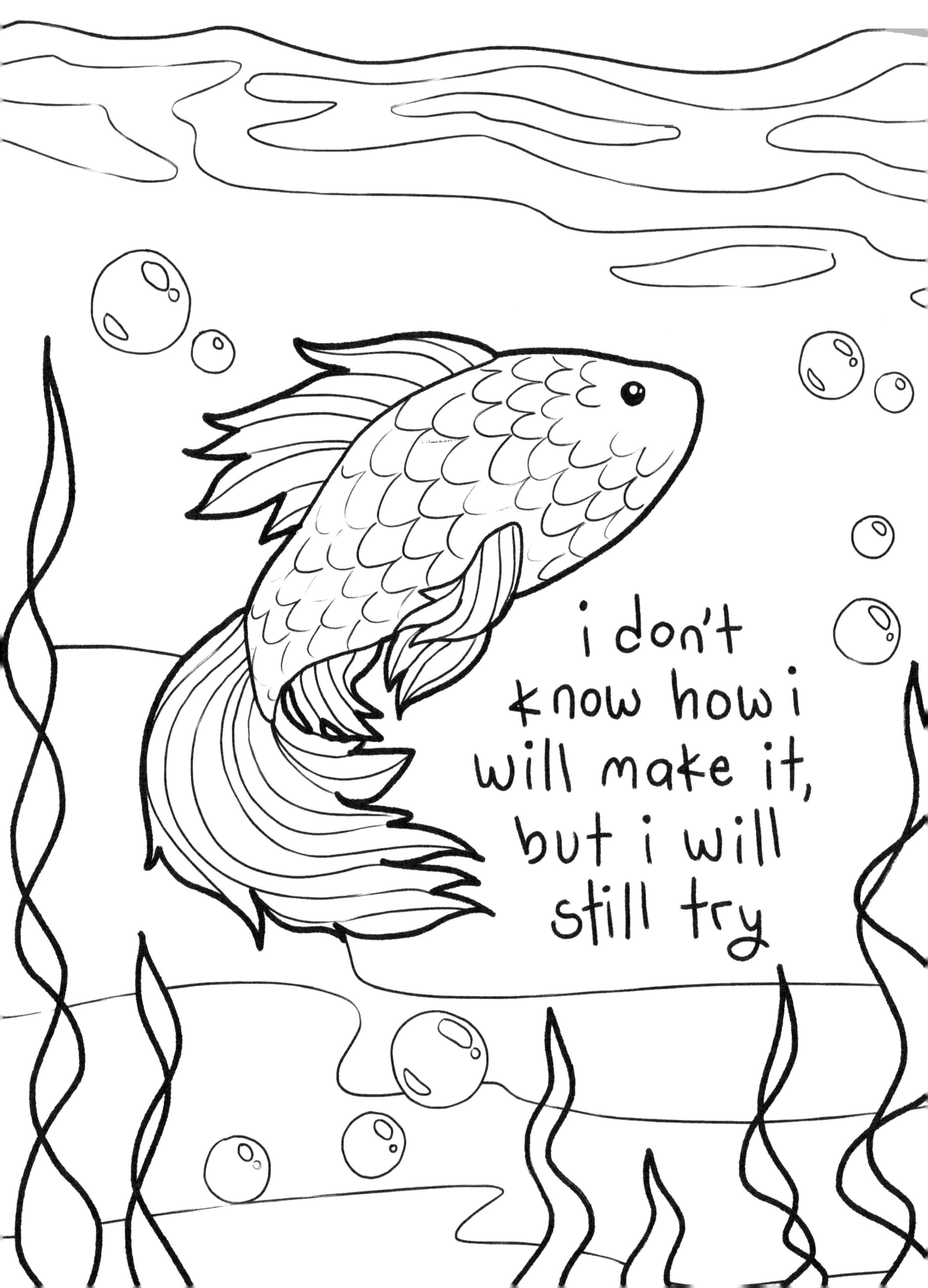
i don't
know how i
will make it,
but i will
still try

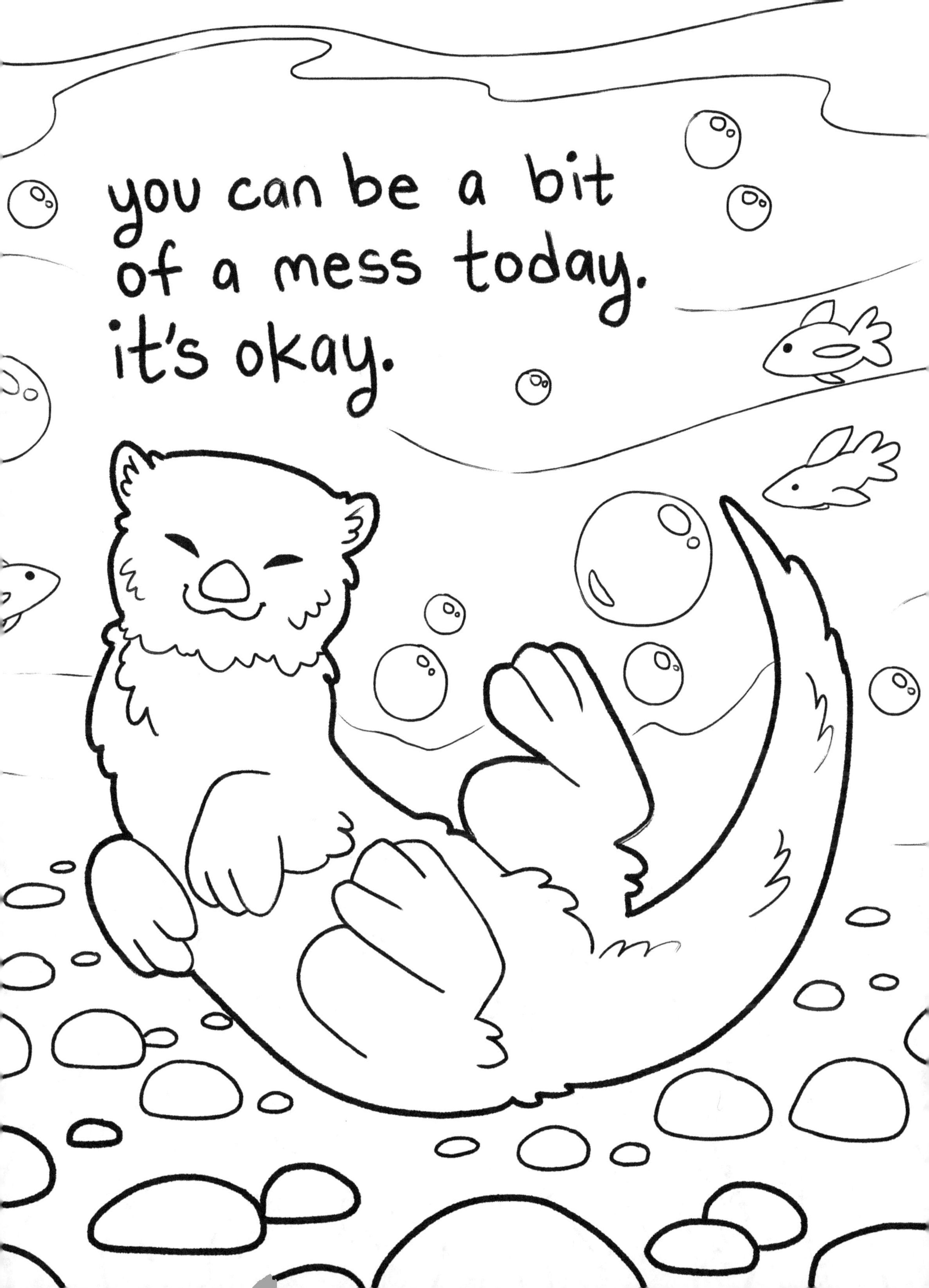
you can be a bit
of a mess today.
it's okay.

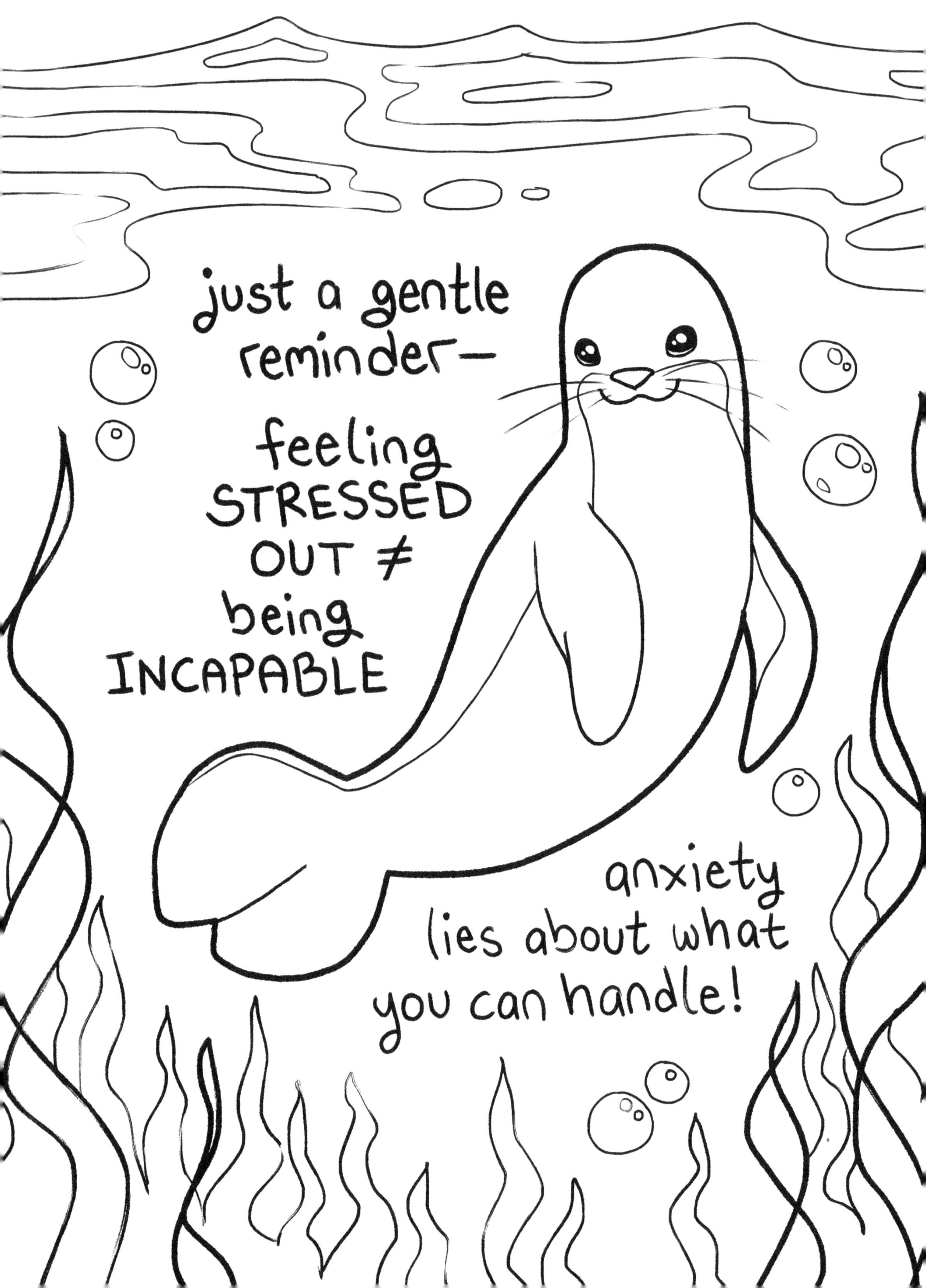
just a gentle reminder—
feeling STRESSED OUT ≠ being INCAPABLE
anxiety lies about what you can handle!

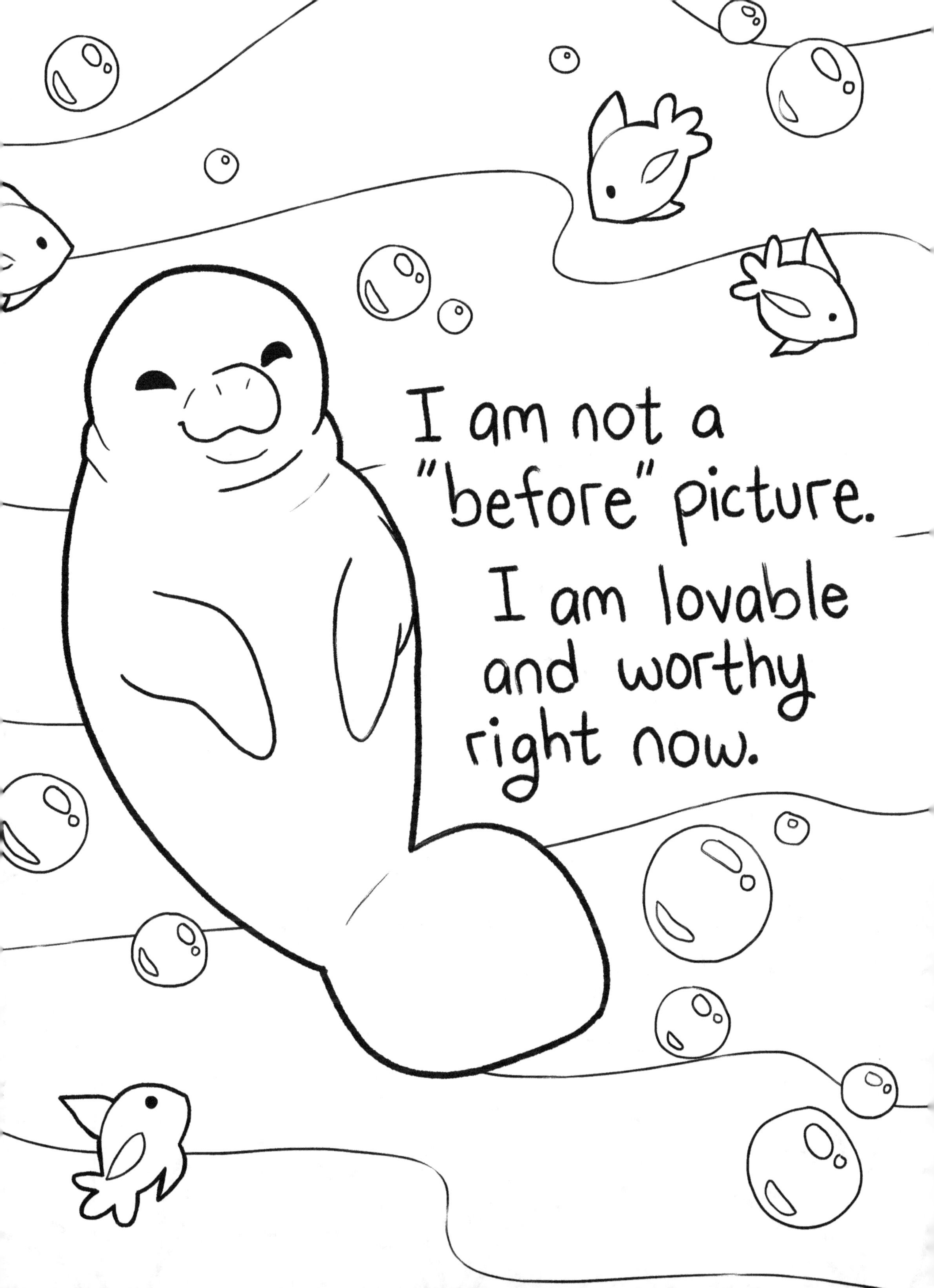
I am not a "before" picture.
I am lovable and worthy right now.

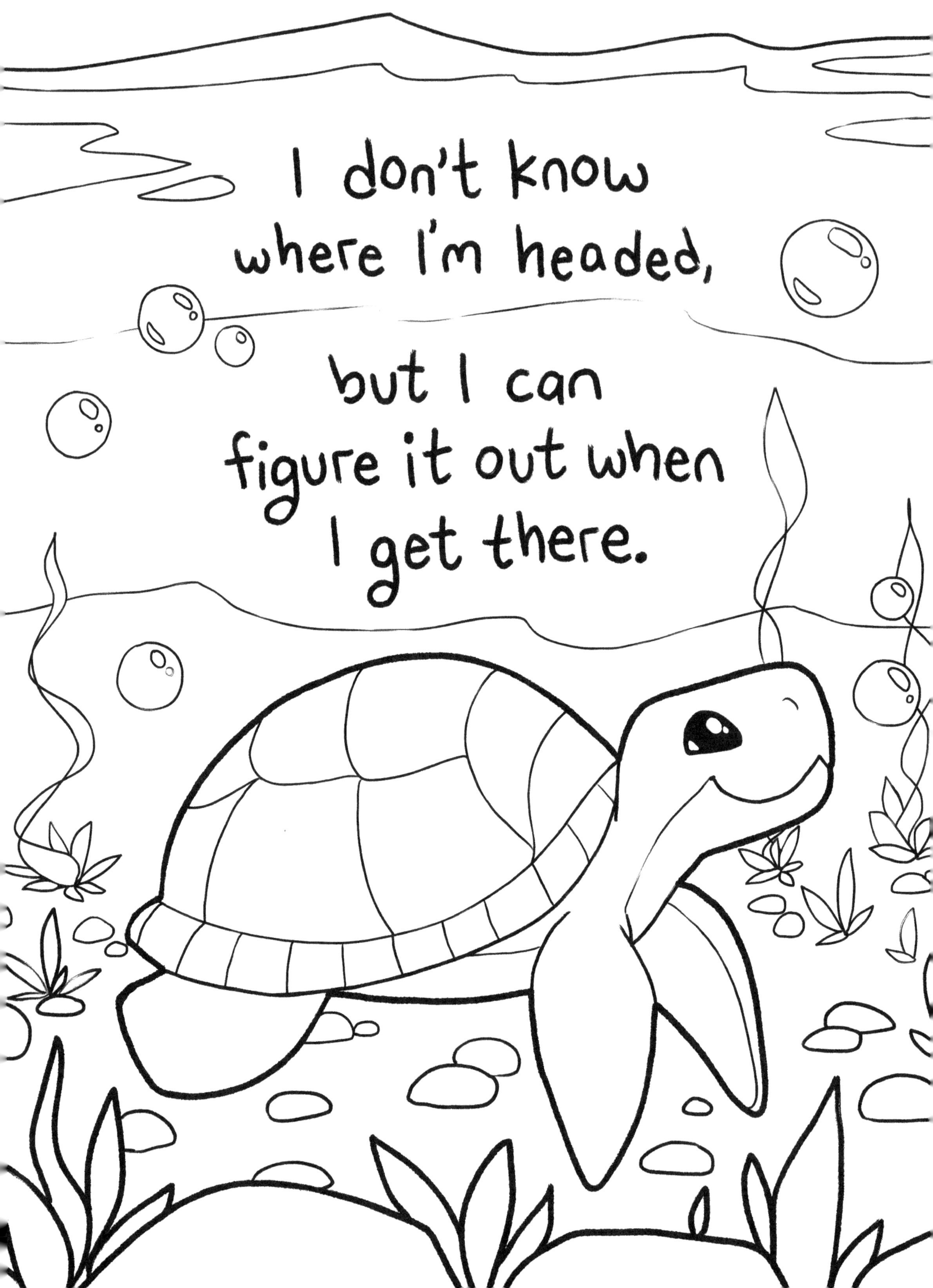
I don't know
where I'm headed,
but I can
figure it out when
I get there.

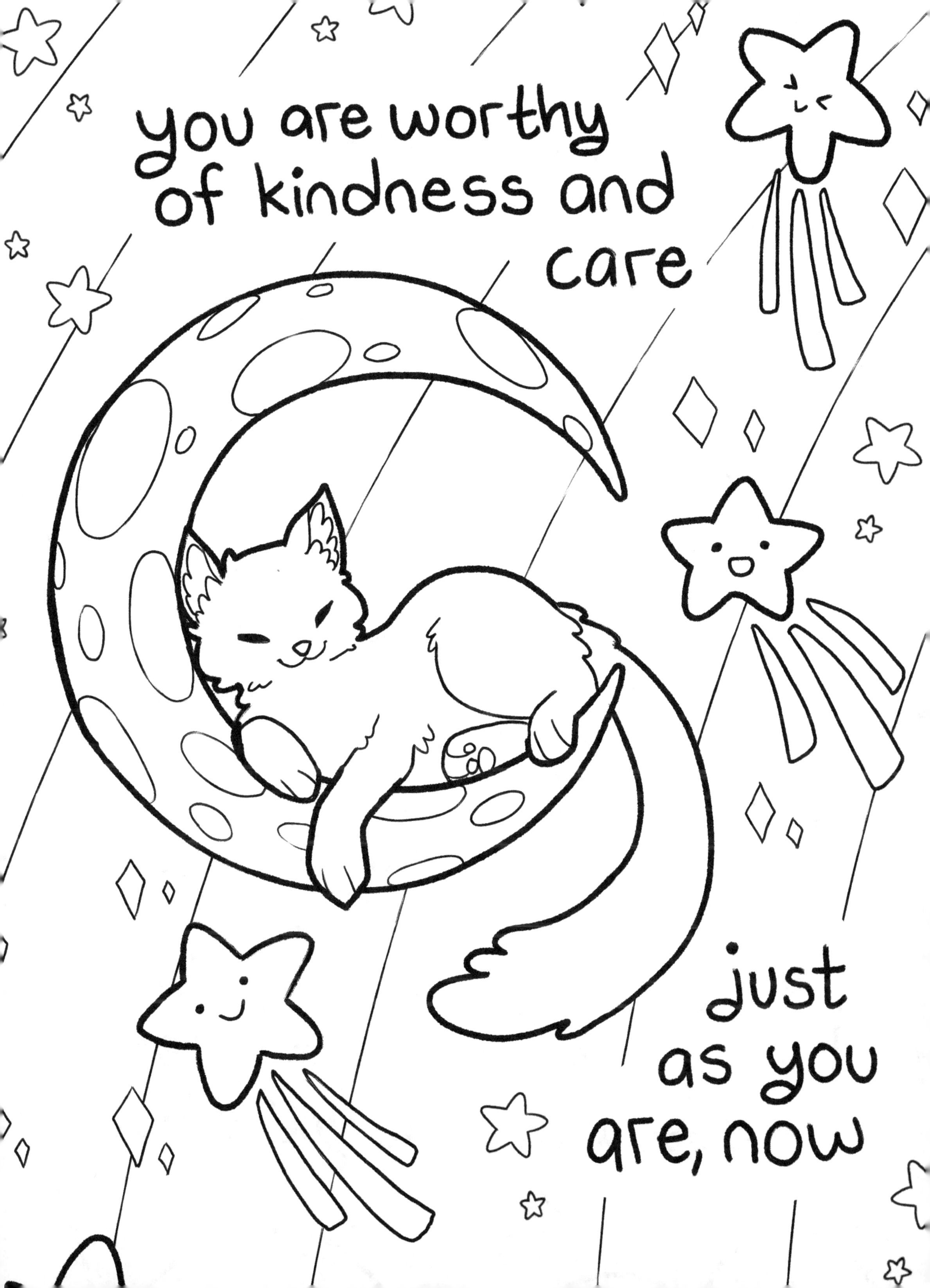

you are worthy of kindness and care

just as you are, now

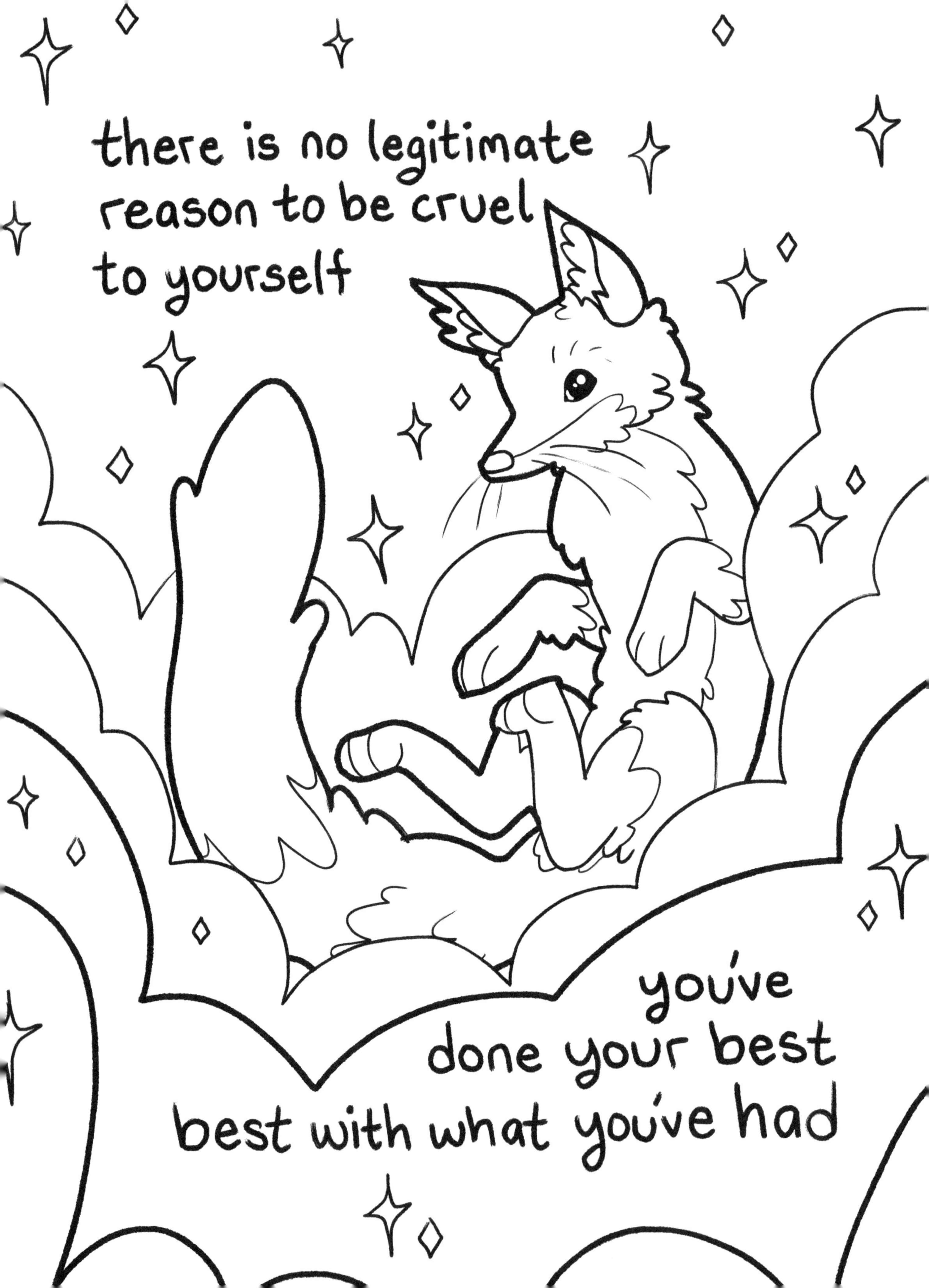
there is no legitimate
reason to be cruel
to yourself
you've
done your best
best with what you've had

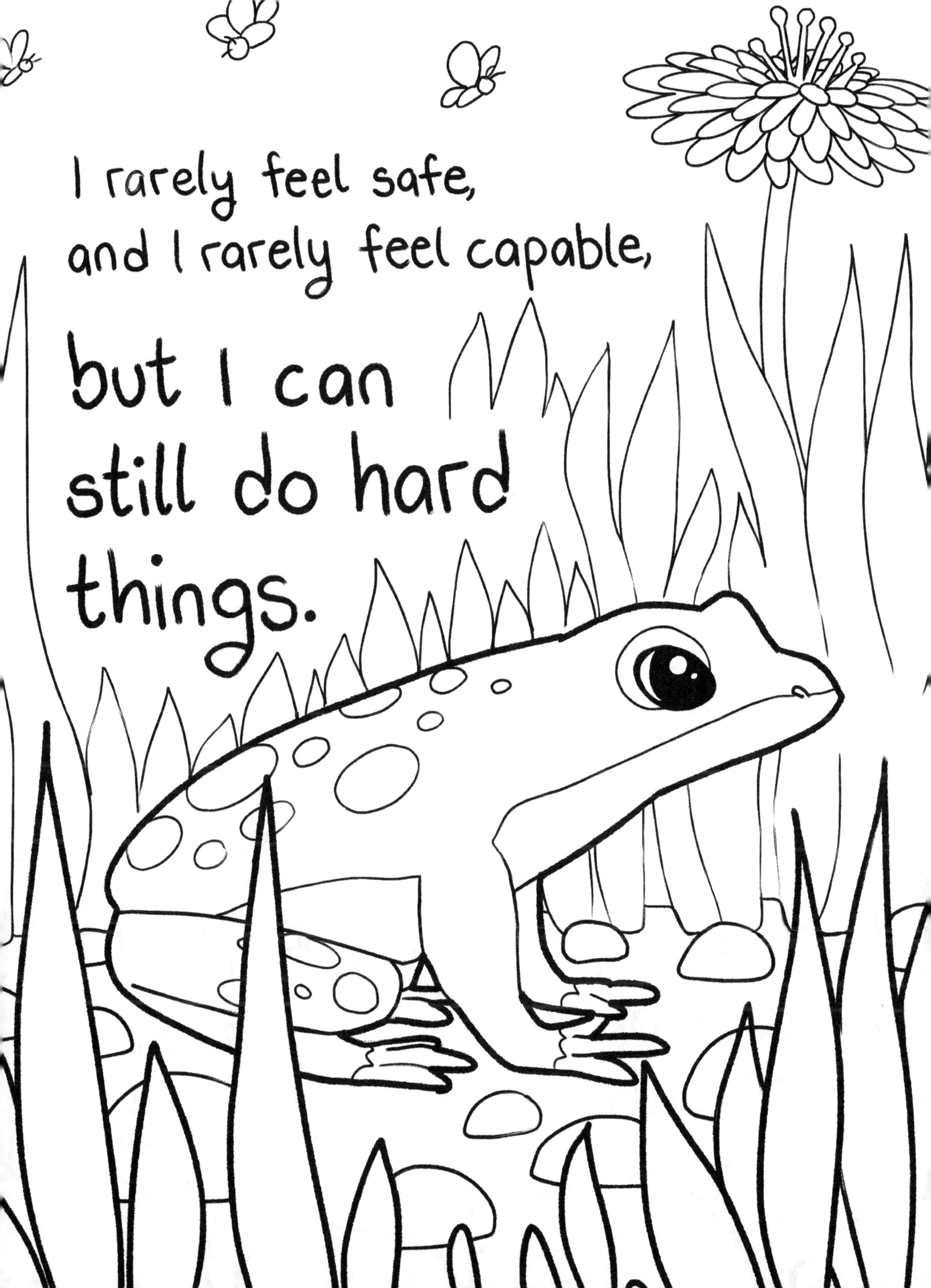
I rarely feel safe,
and I rarely feel capable,
but I can
still do hard
things.

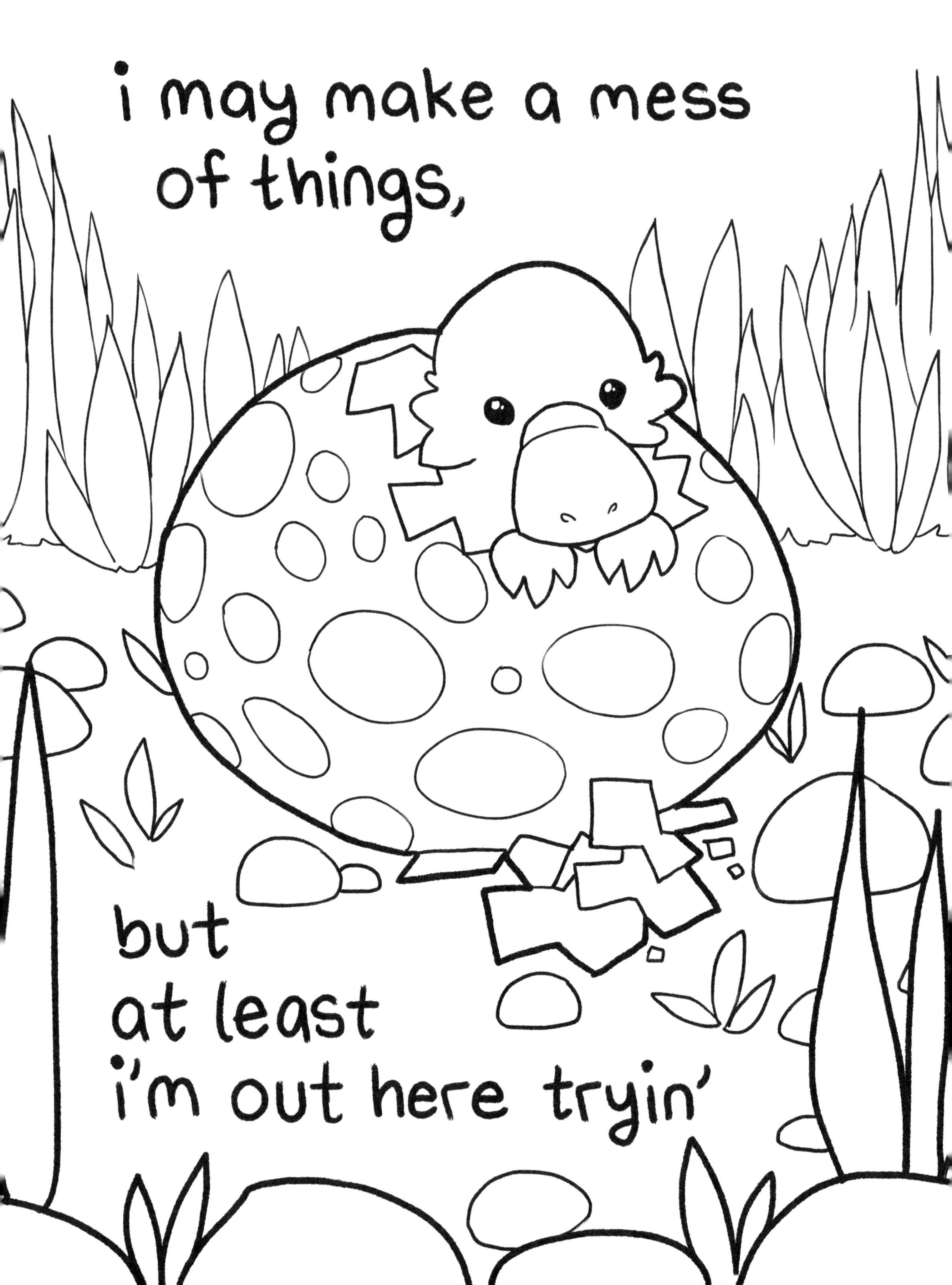
i may make a mess
of things,
but
at least
i'm out here tryin'

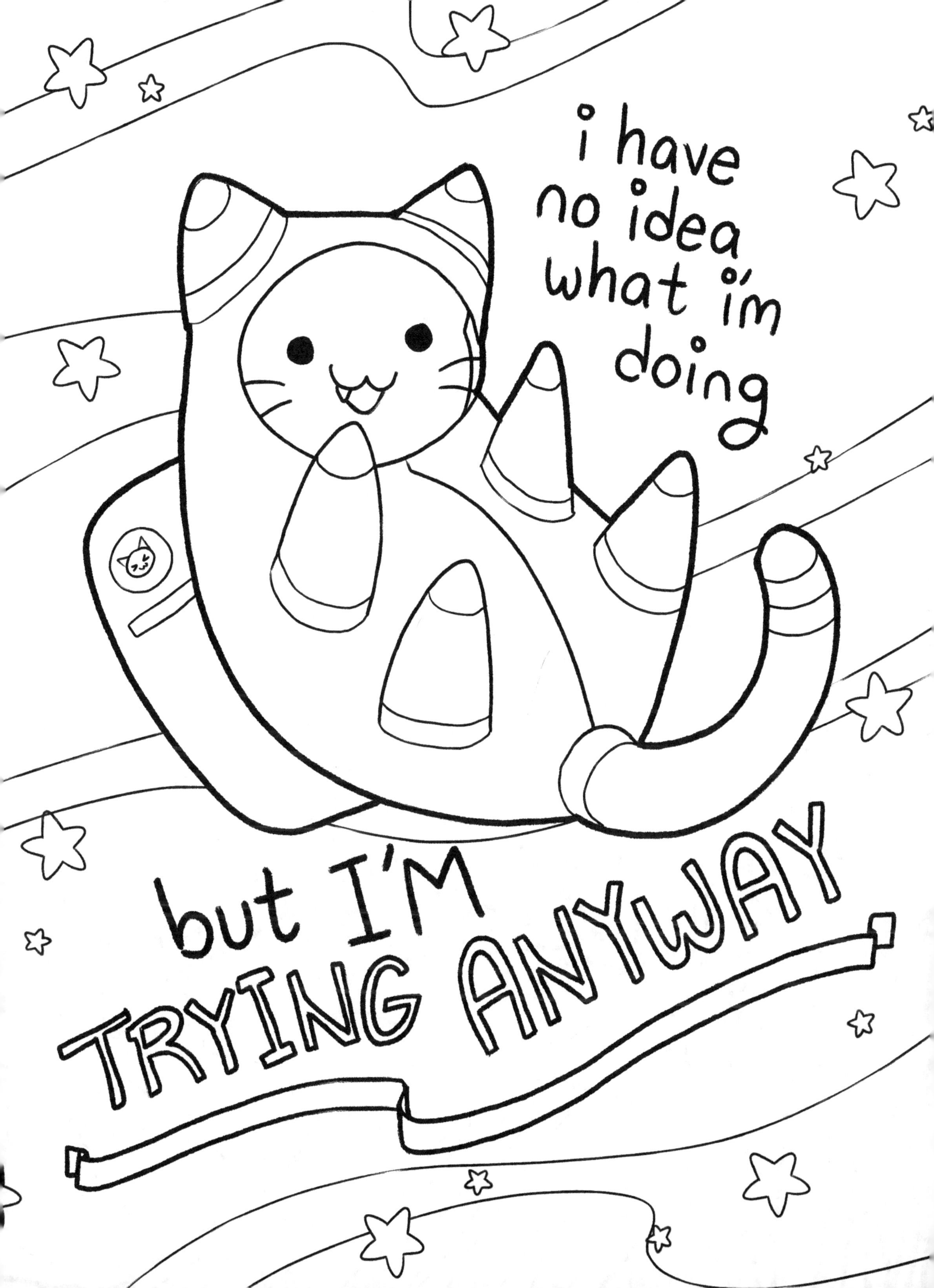
i have no idea what i'm doing
but I'M TRYING ANYWAY

It's okay
to just muddle
through right now.
"Good enough" is,
in fact, good
enough.

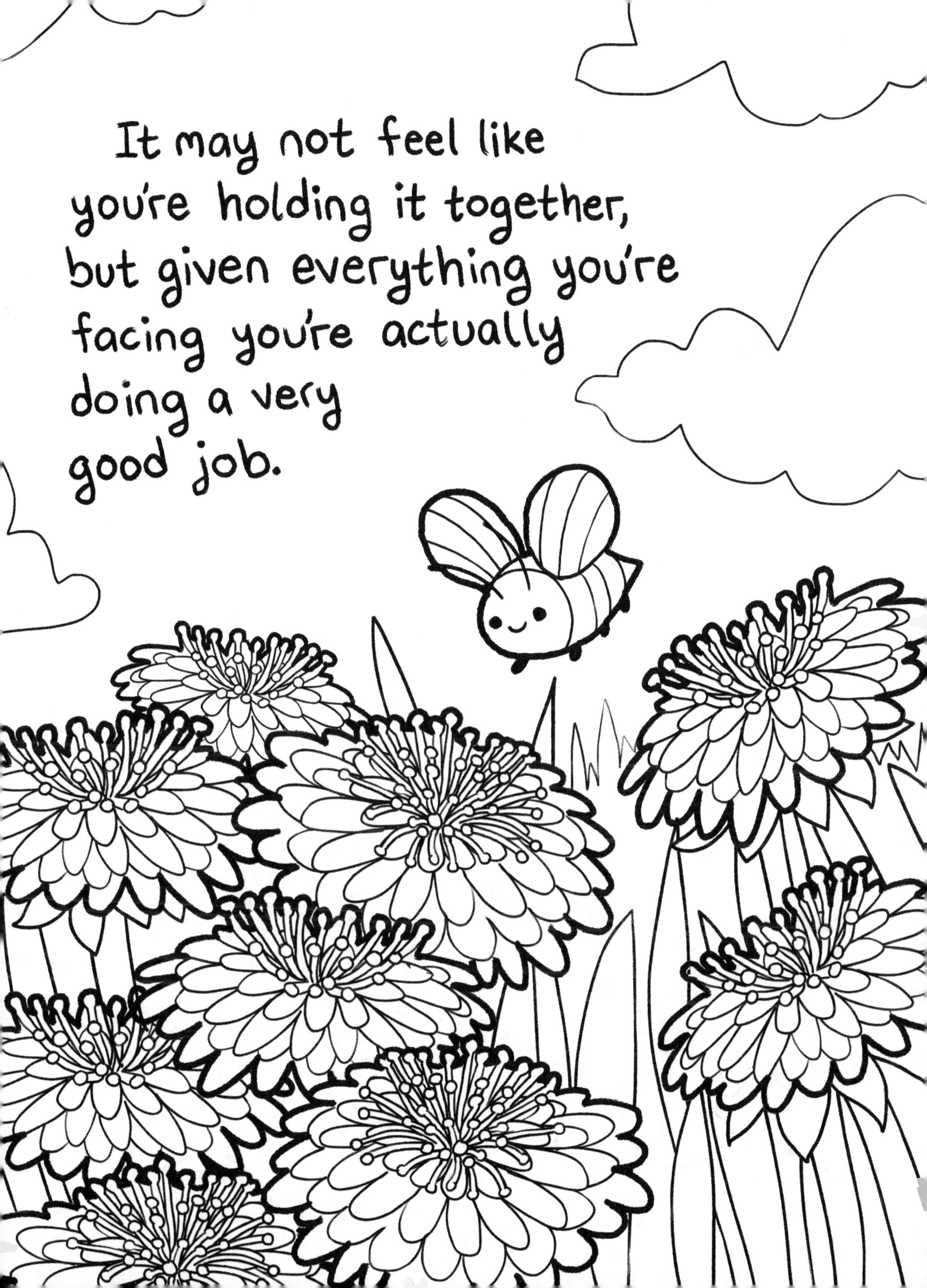
It may not feel like
you're holding it together,
but given everything you're
facing you're actually
doing a very
good job.

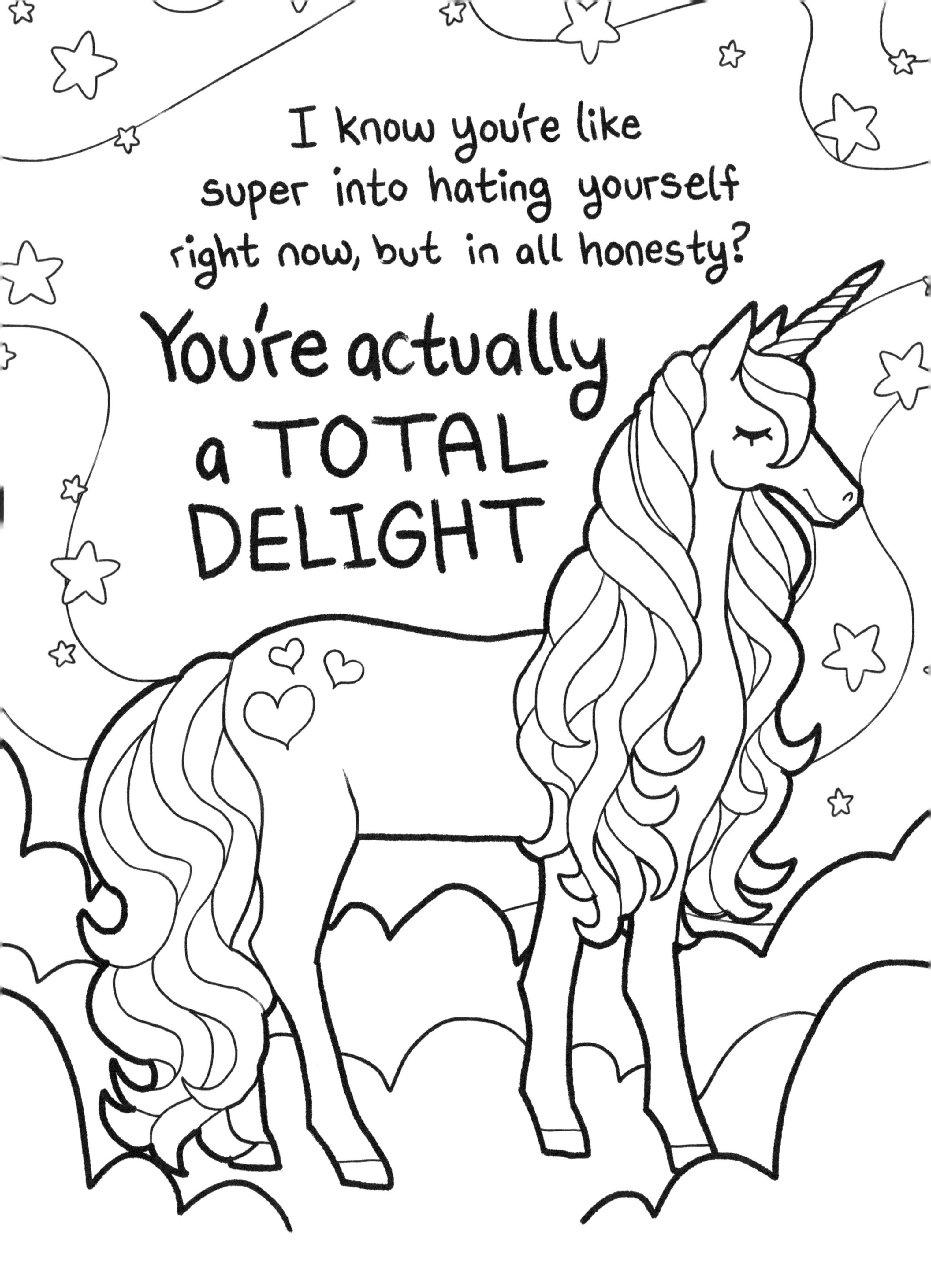
I know you're like
super into hating yourself
right now, but in all honesty?
You're actually
a TOTAL
DELIGHT

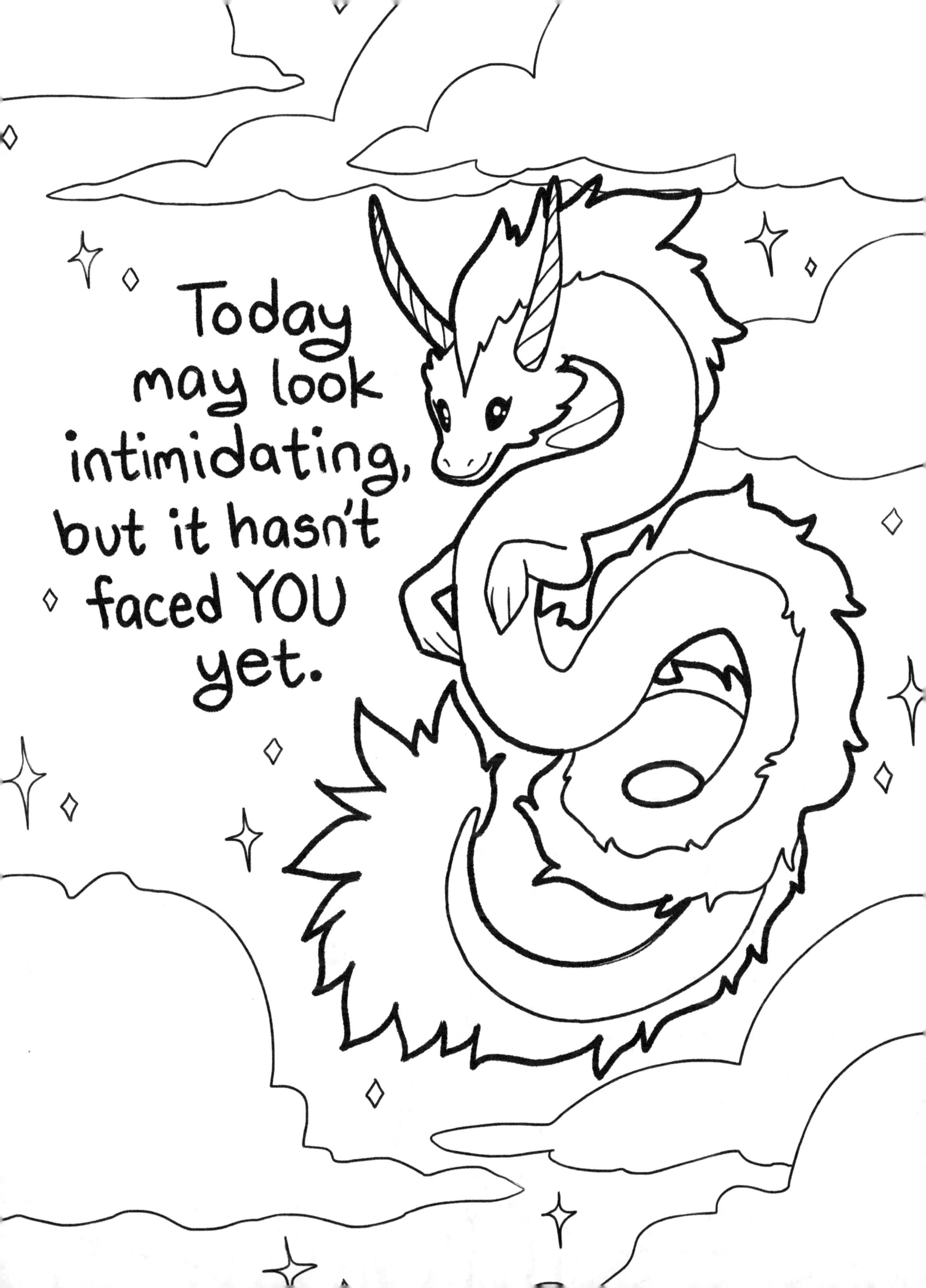
Today may look intimidating, but it hasn't faced YOU yet.

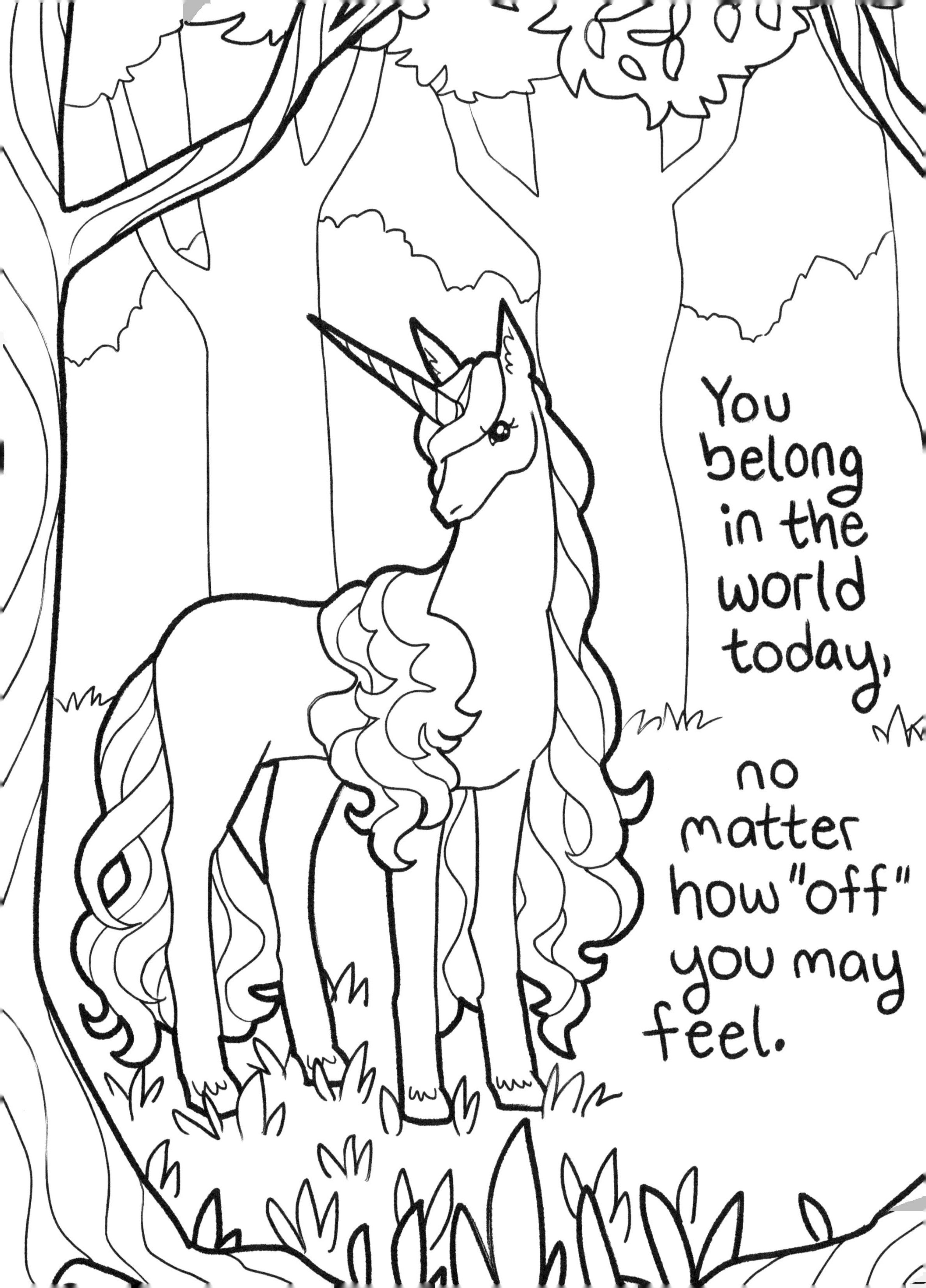

You
belong
in the
world
today,

no
matter
how "off"
you may
feel.

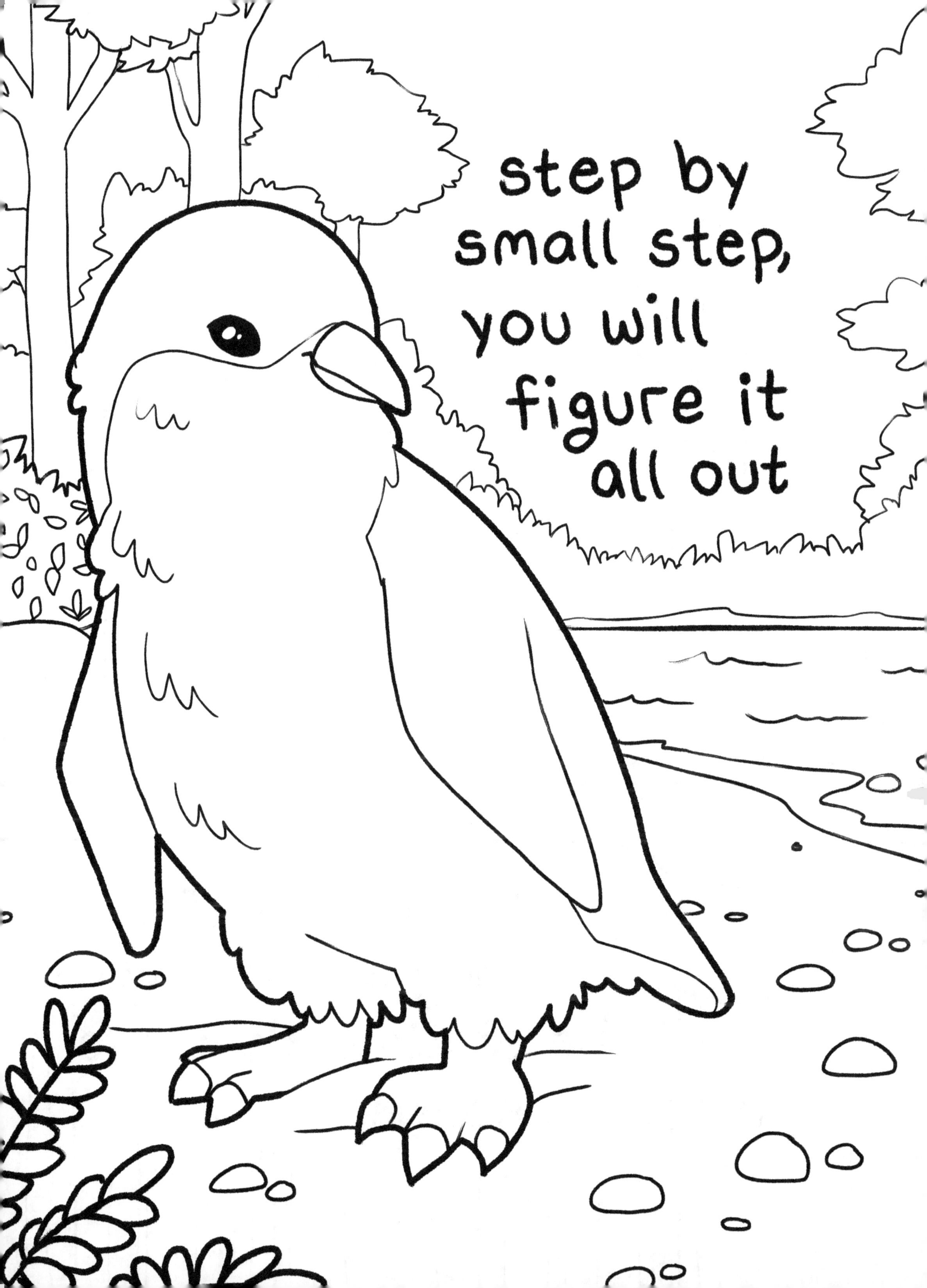

step by
small step,
you will
figure it
all out

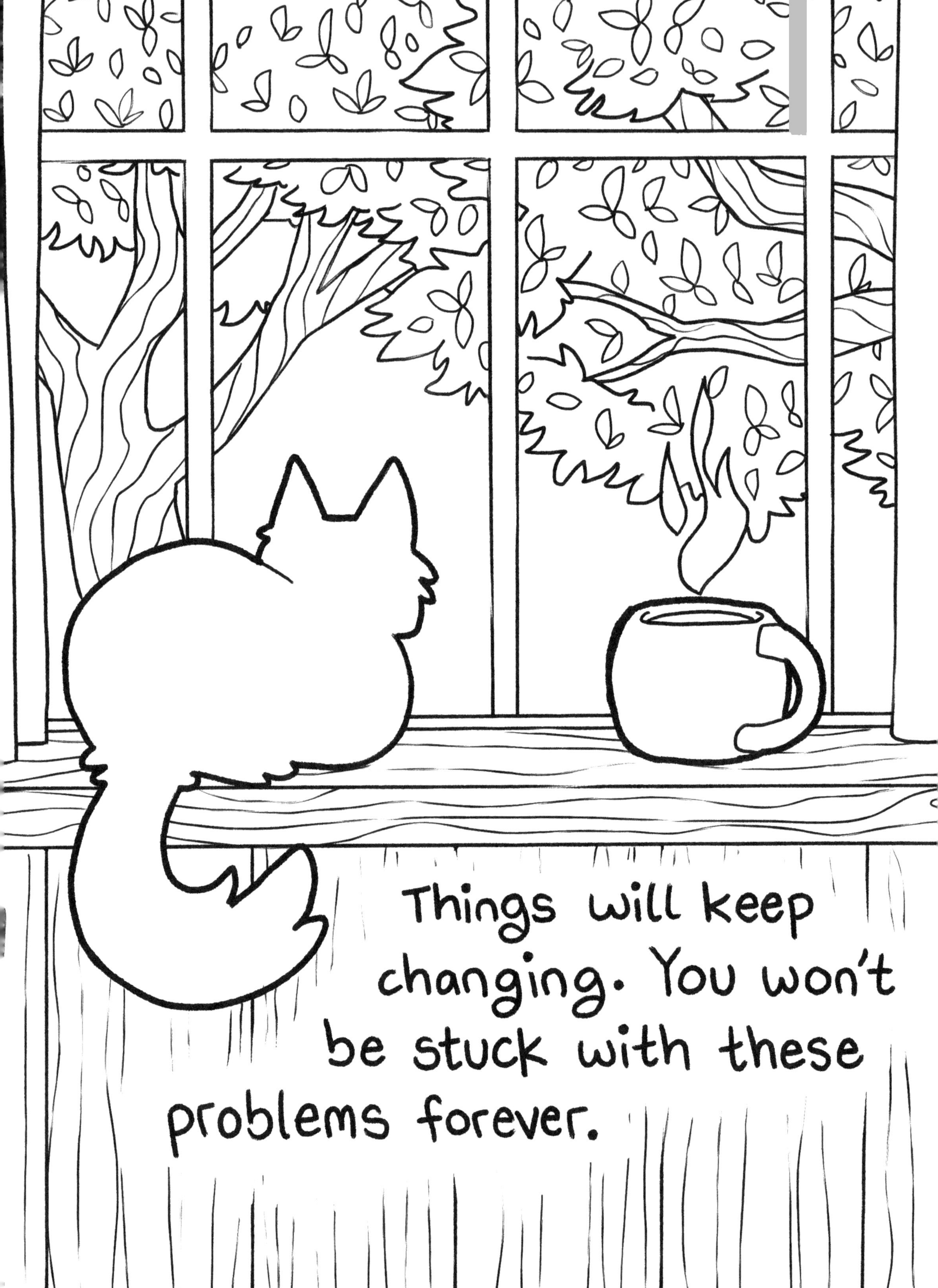
Things will keep changing. You won't be stuck with these problems forever.

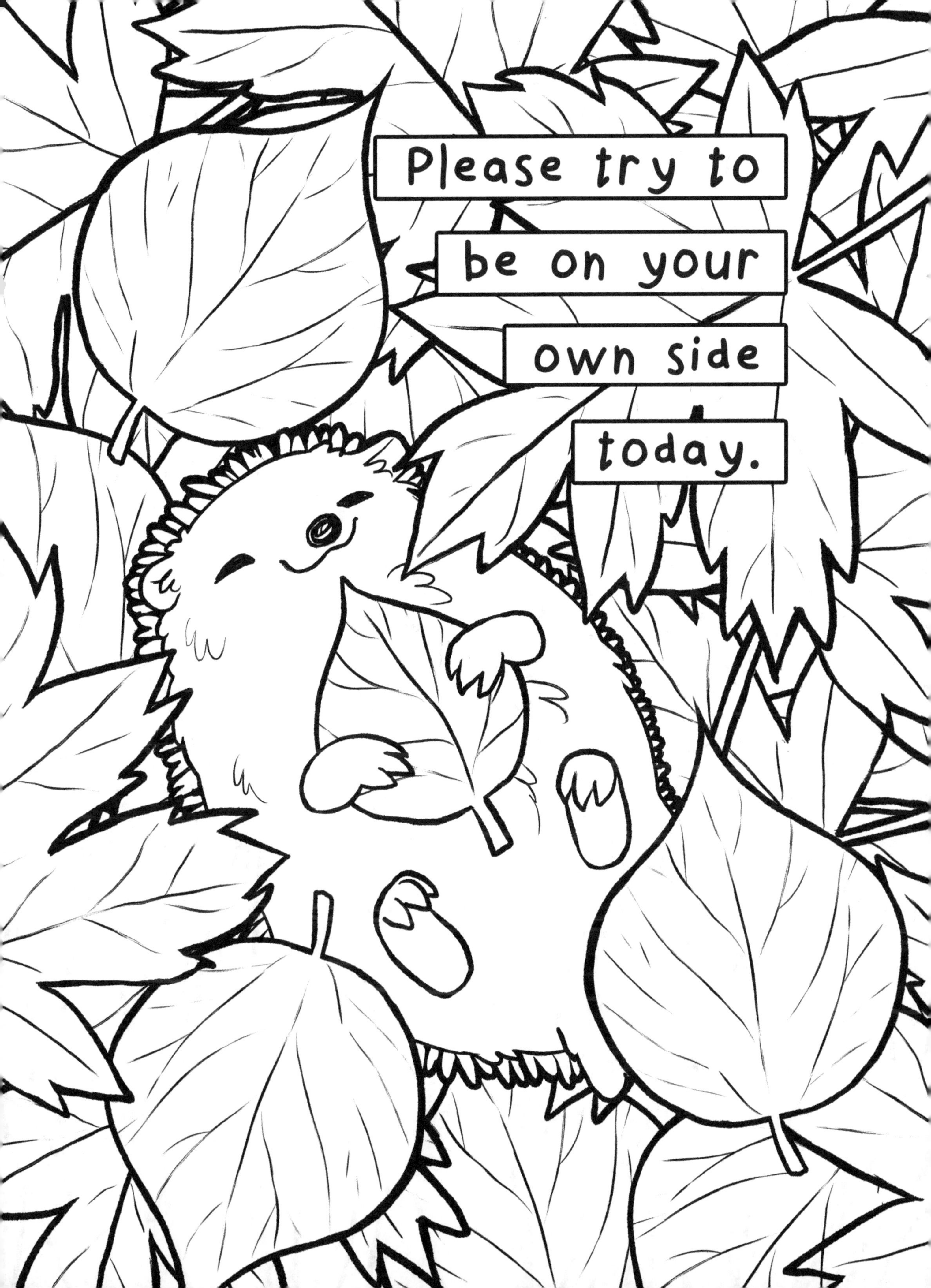
Please try to
be on your
own side
today.

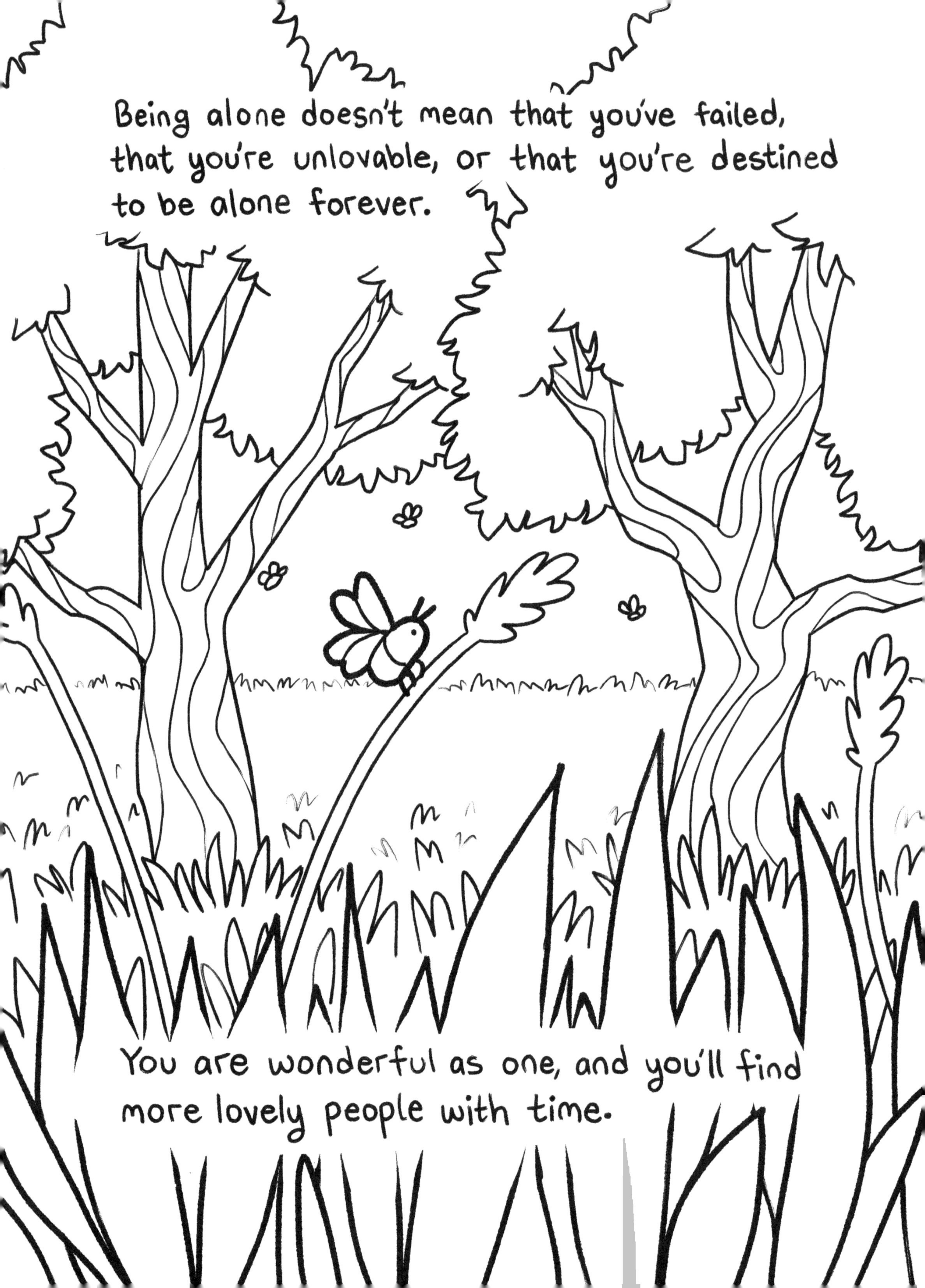

Being alone doesn't mean that you've failed, that you're unlovable, or that you're destined to be alone forever.

You are wonderful as one, and you'll find more lovely people with time.

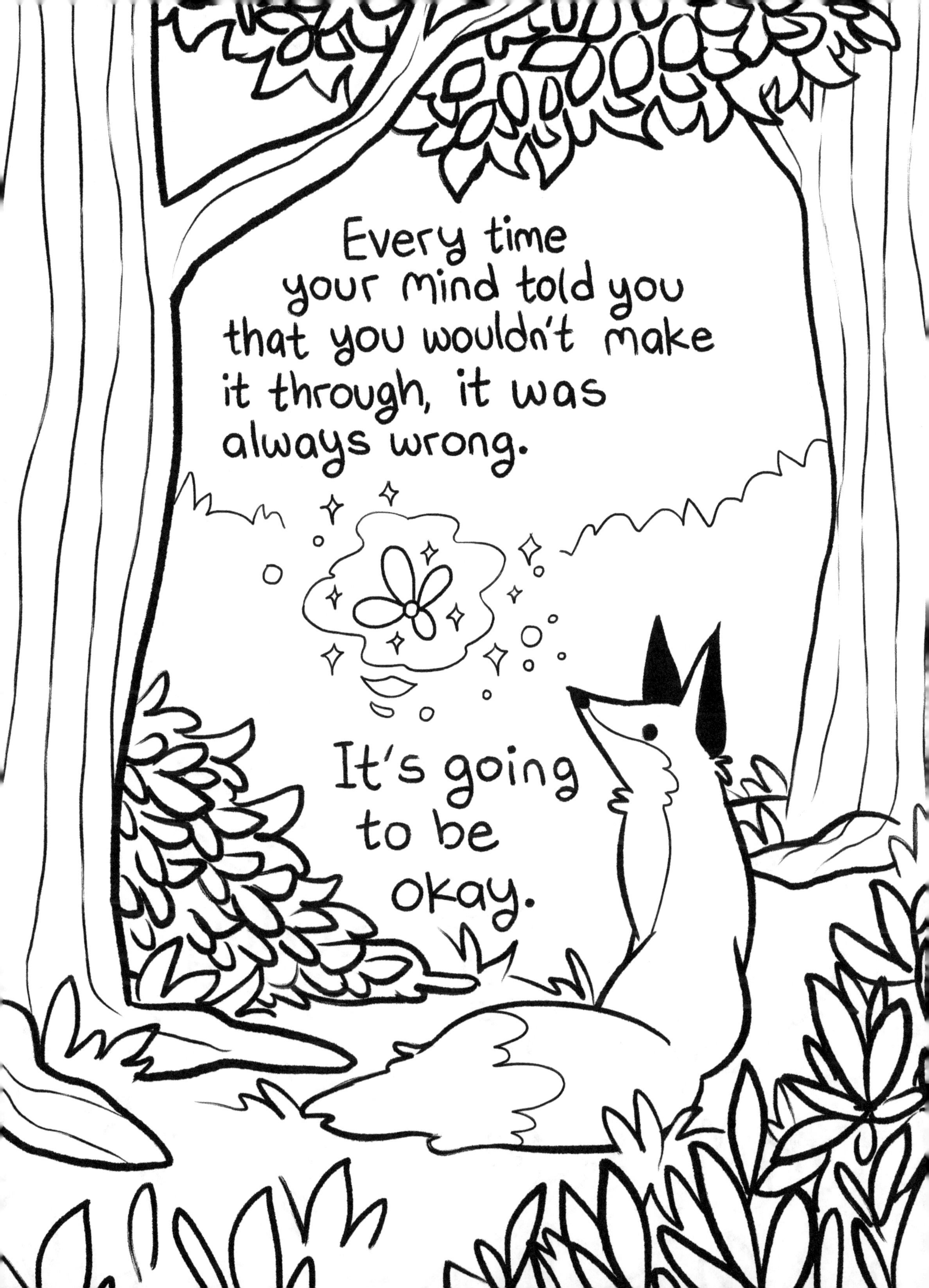
Every time
your mind told you
that you wouldn't make
it through, it was
always wrong.
It's going
to be
okay.

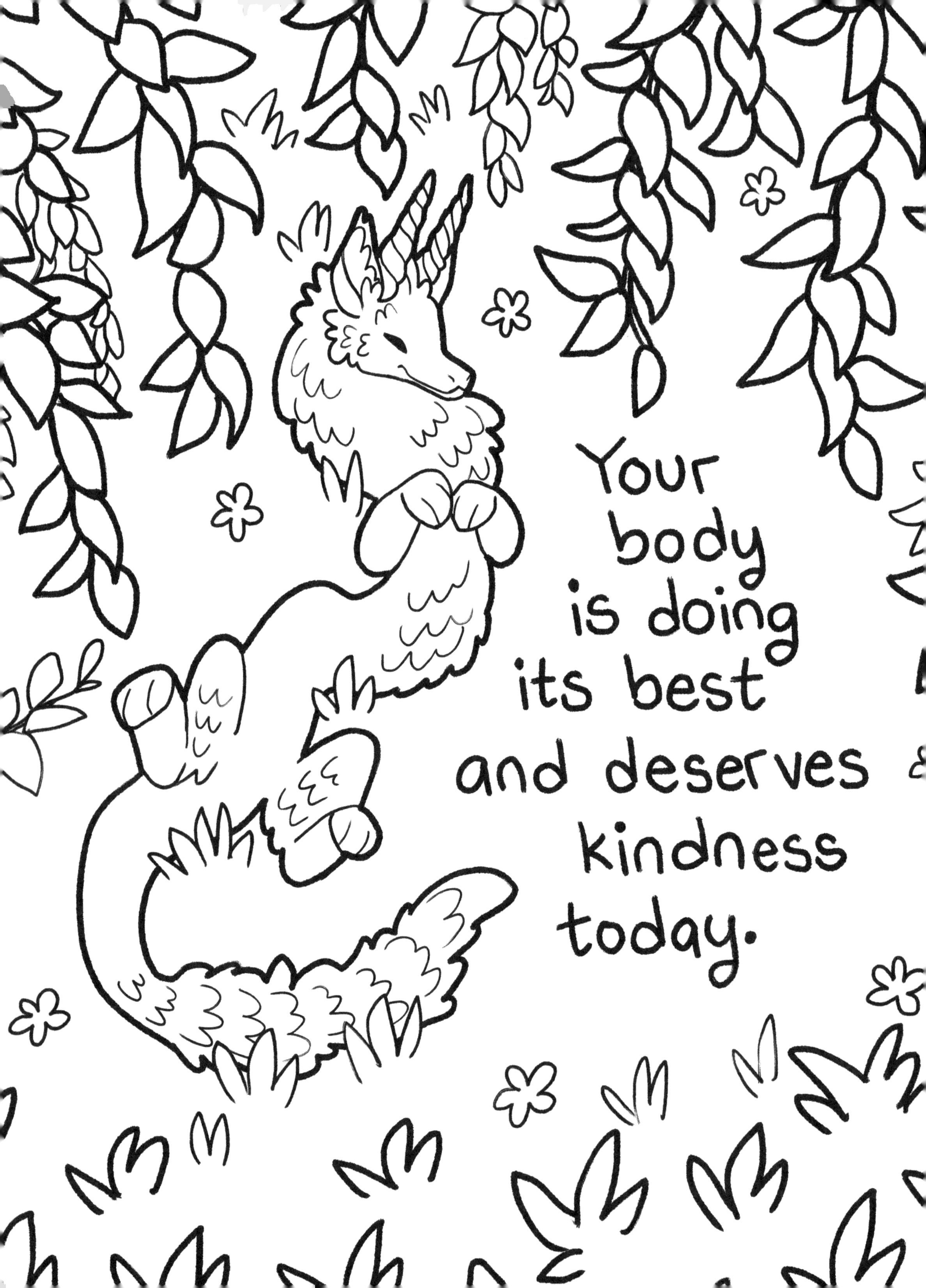
Your body is doing its best and deserves kindness today.

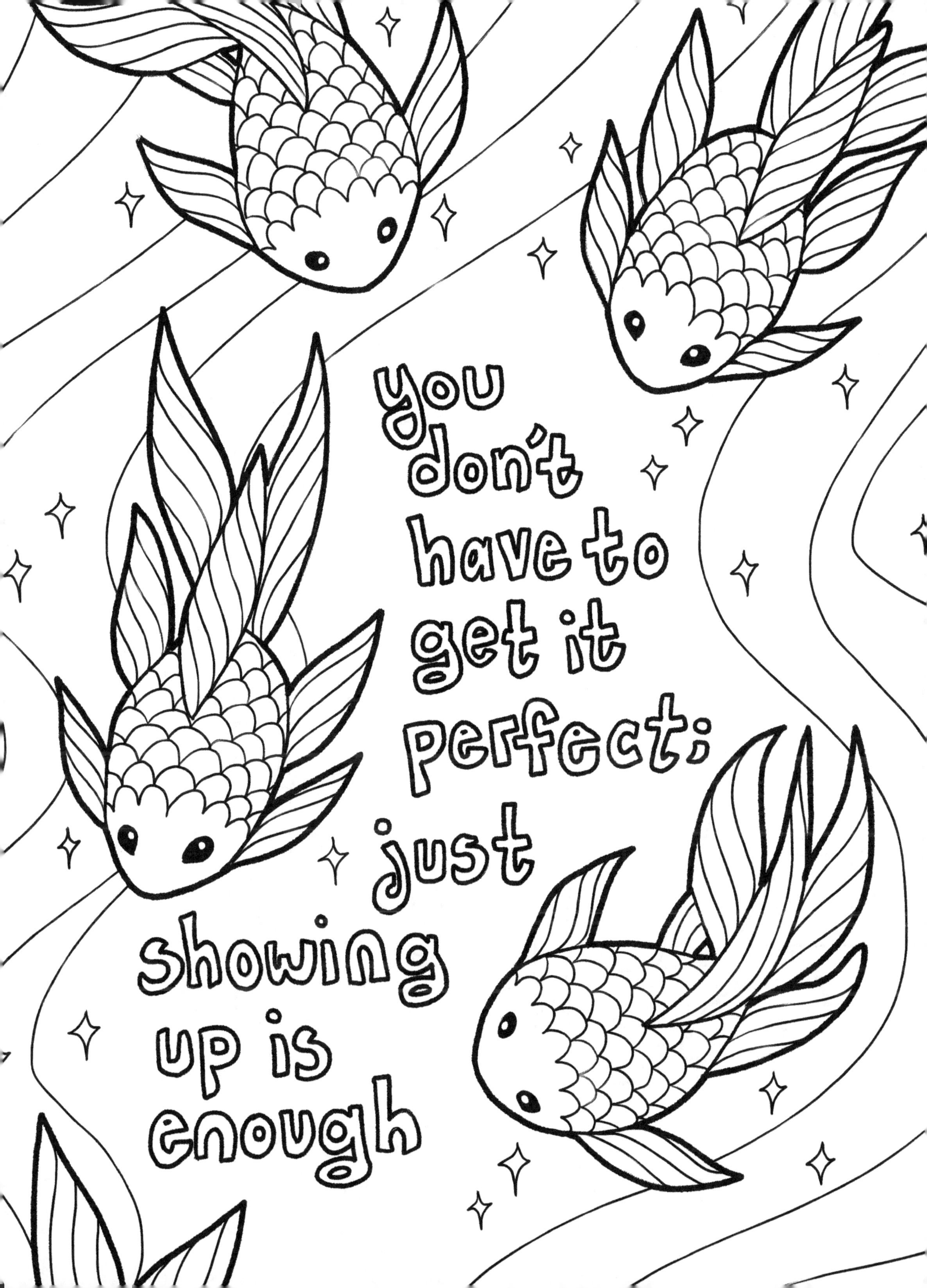
you
don't
have to
get it
perfect;
just
showing
up is
enough

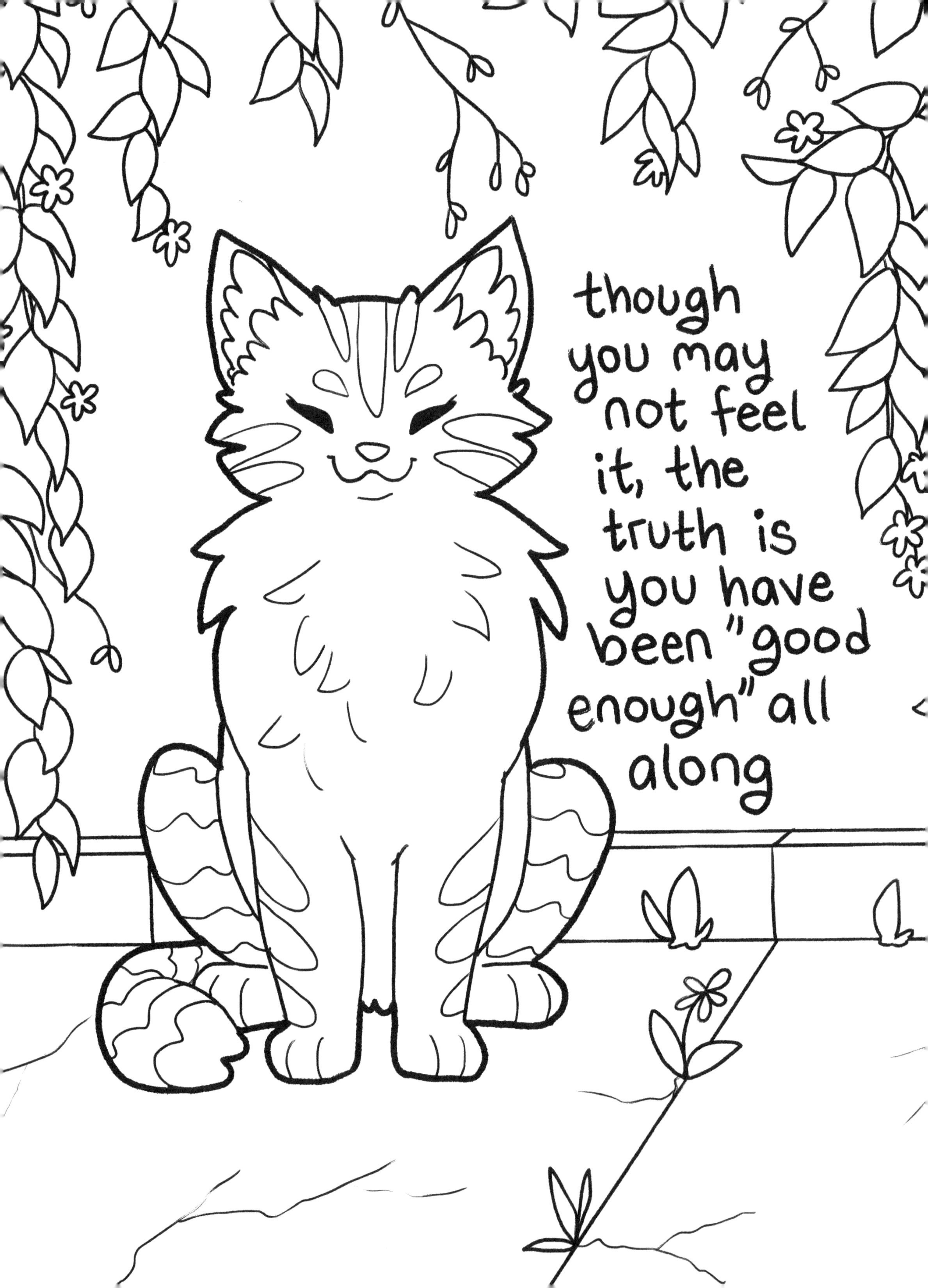

though
you may
not feel
it, the
truth is
you have
been "good
enough" all
along

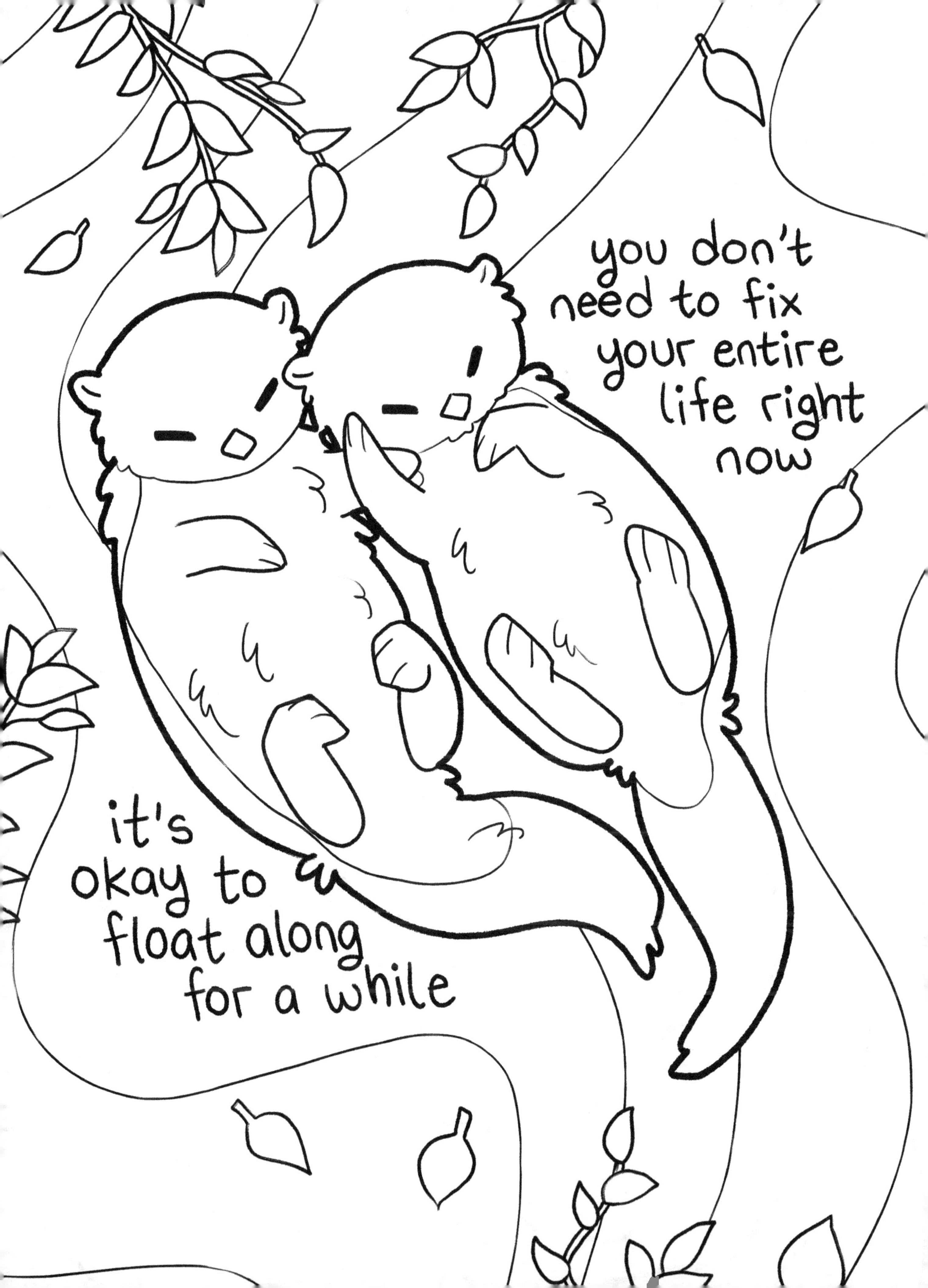

you don't
need to fix
your entire
life right
now

it's
okay to
float along
for a while

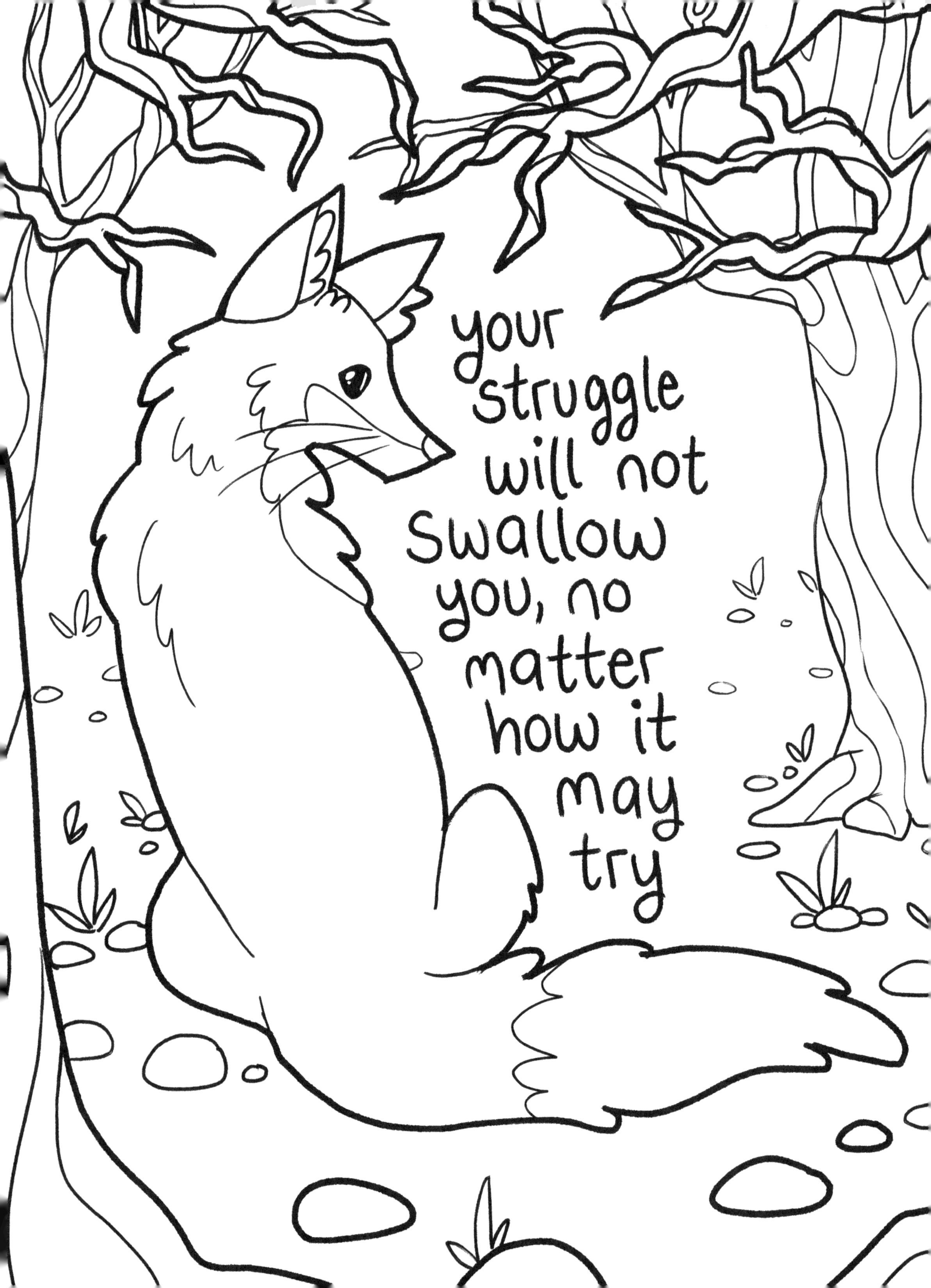
your
struggle
will not
swallow
you, no
matter
how it
may
try

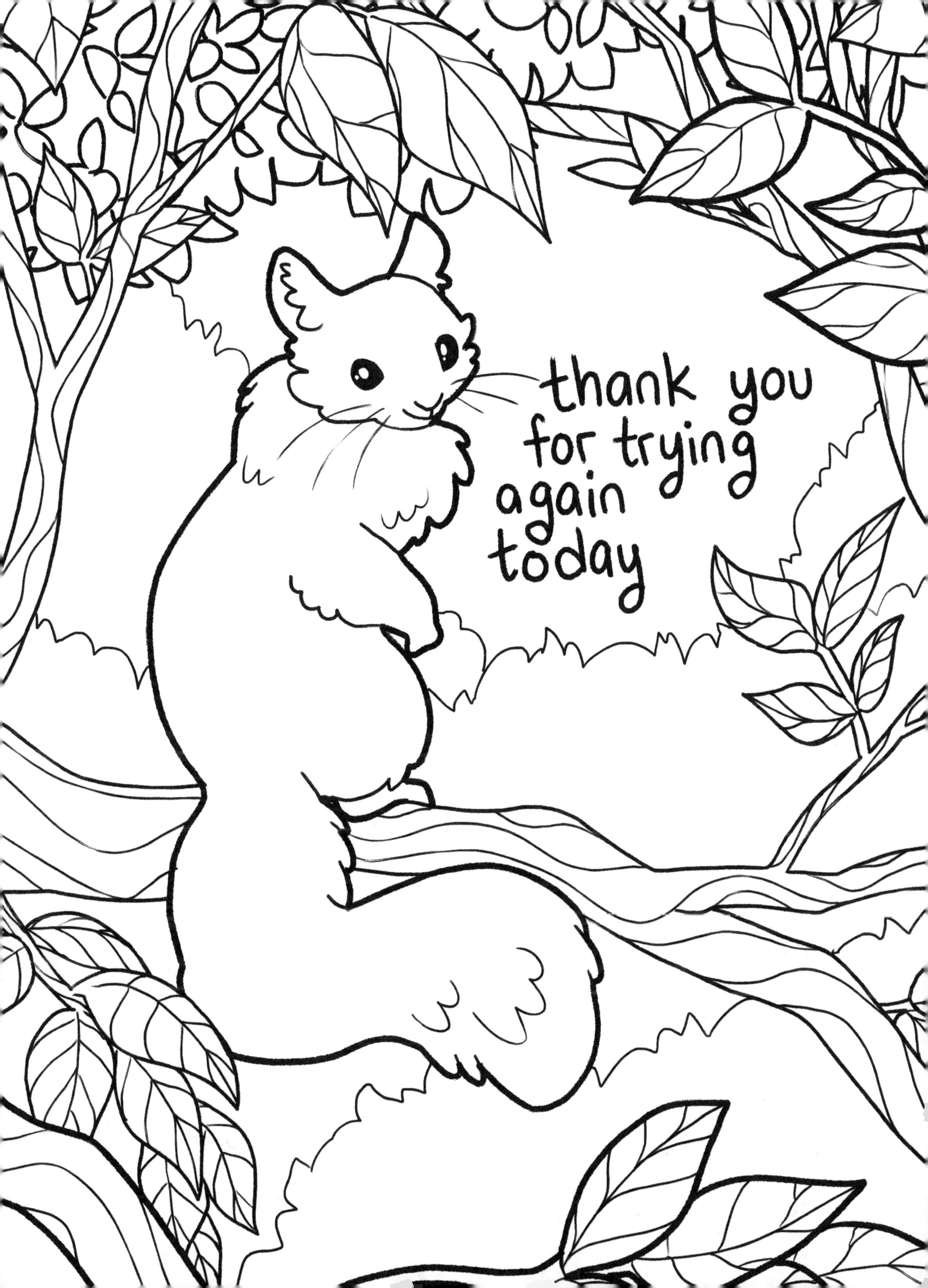
thank you
for trying
again
today

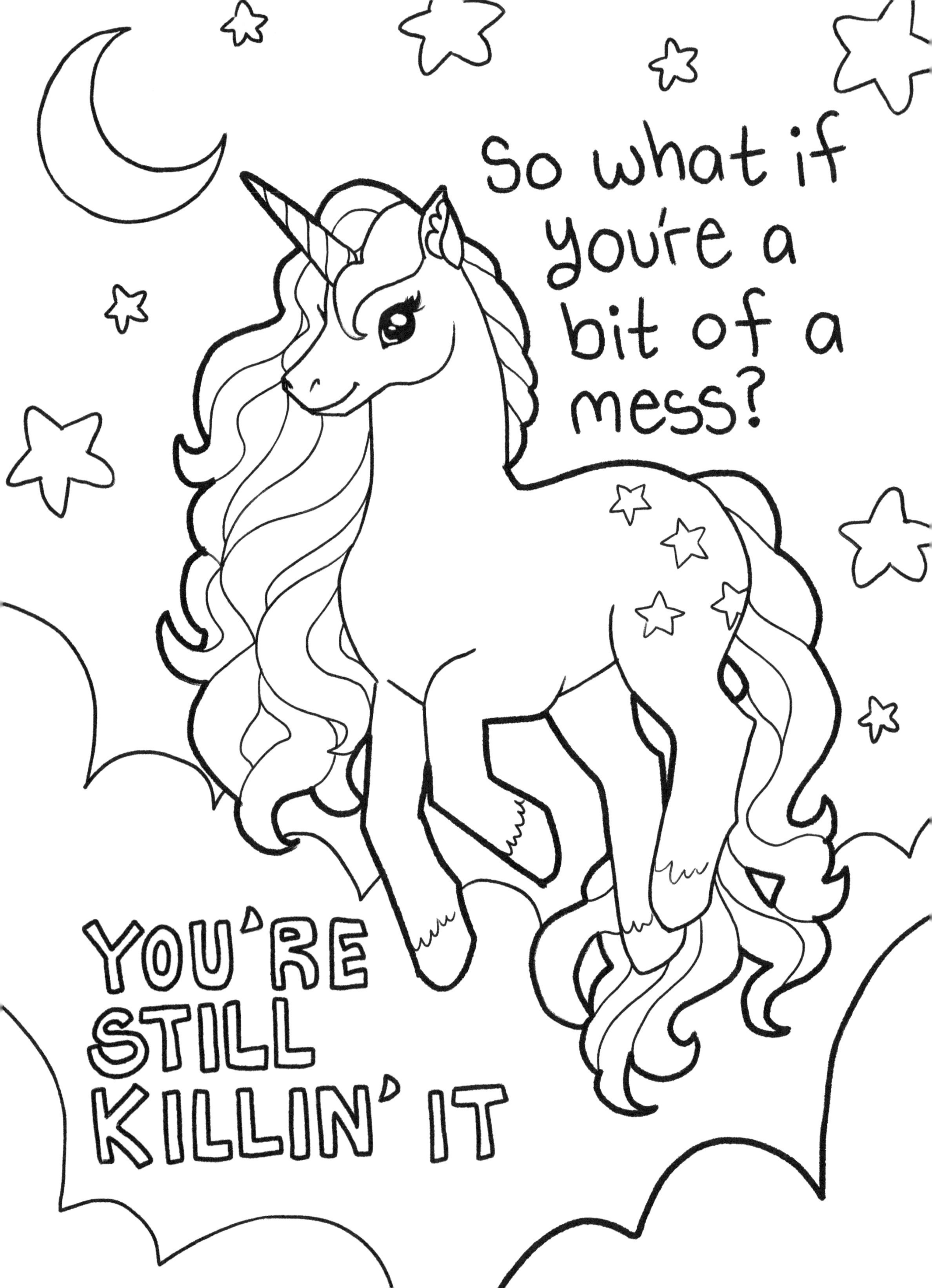
So what if you're a bit of a mess?
YOU'RE STILL KILLIN' IT

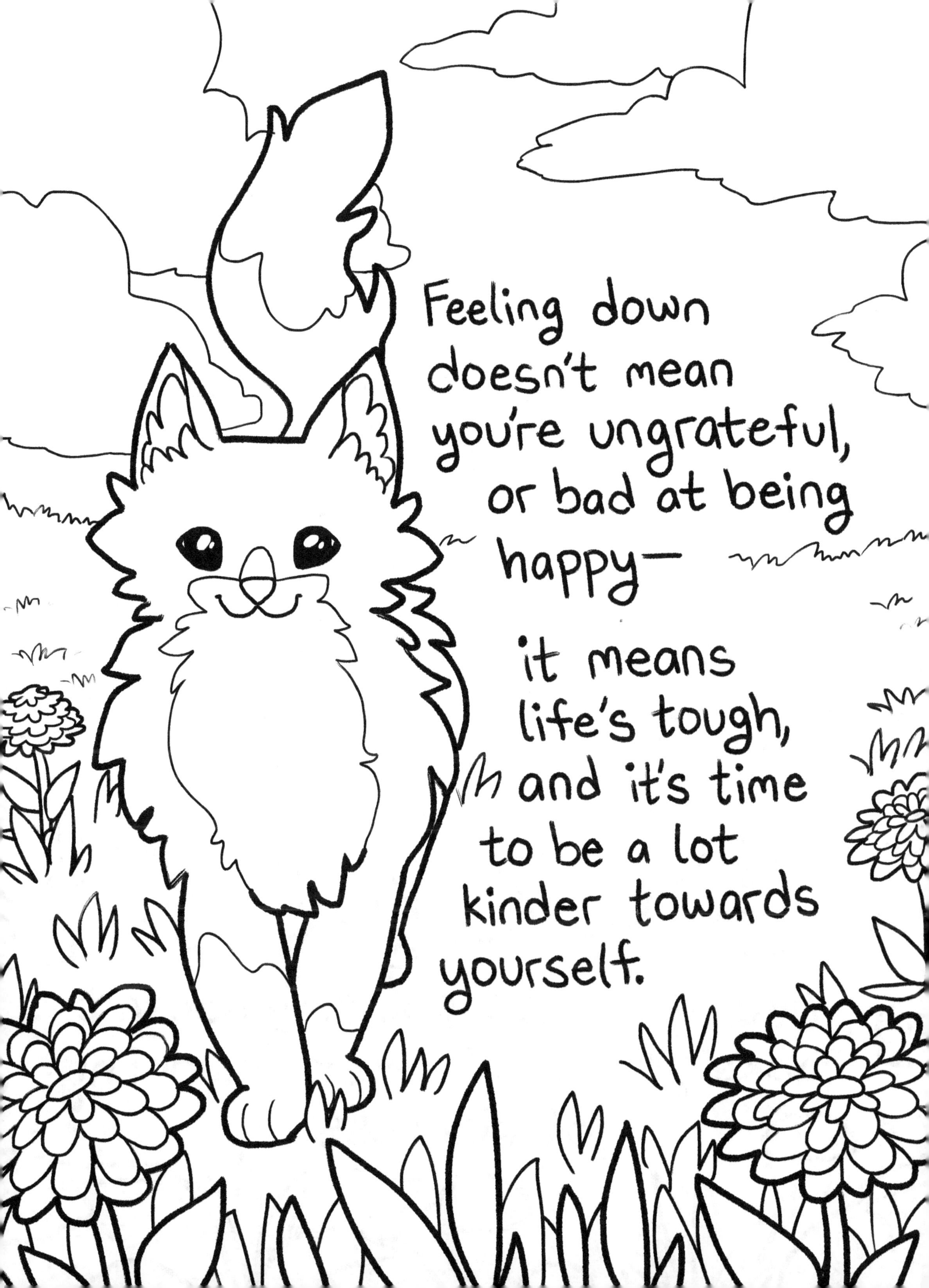

Feeling down
doesn't mean
you're ungrateful,
or bad at being
happy—

it means
life's tough,
and it's time
to be a lot
kinder towards
yourself.

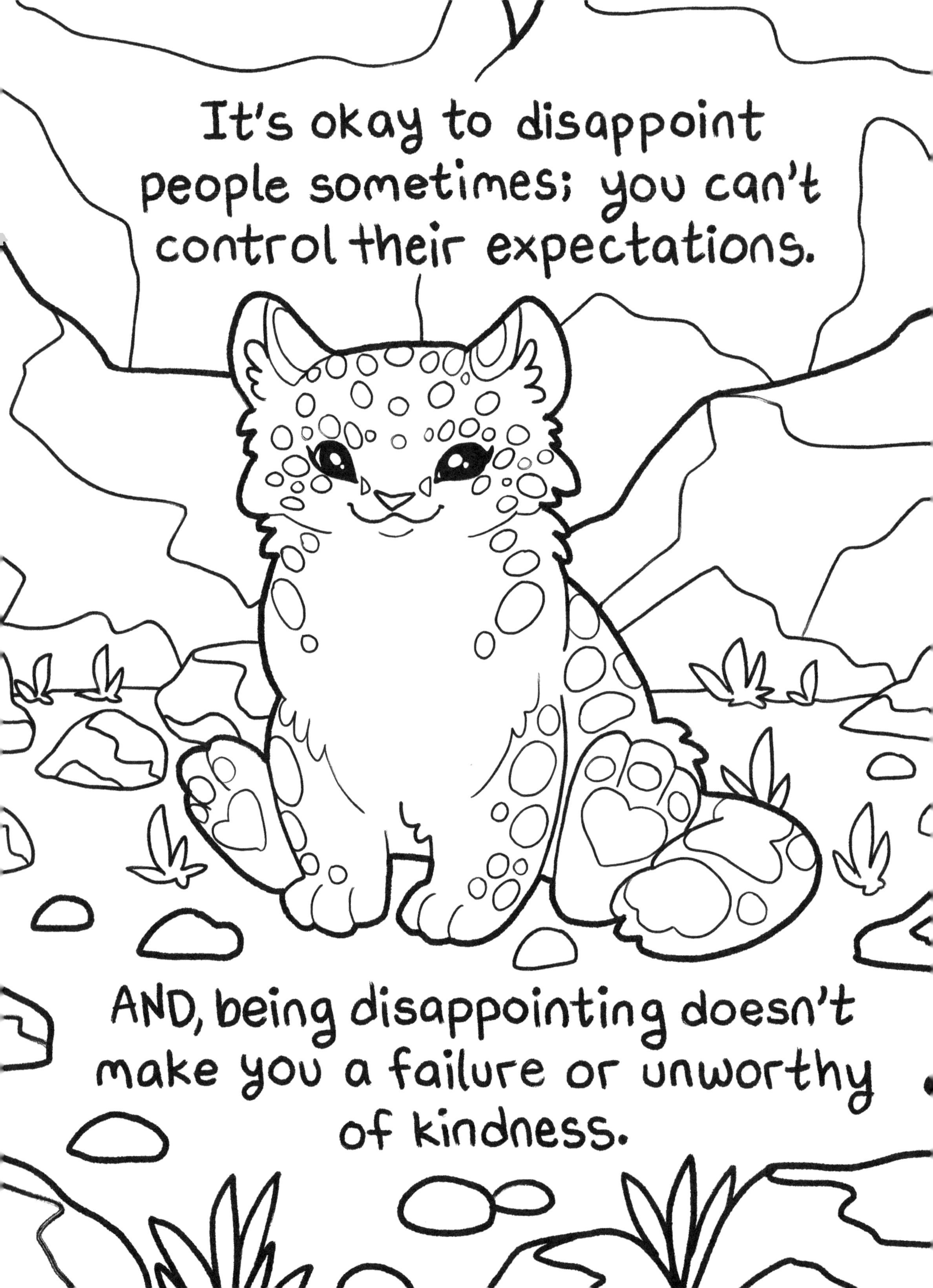
It's okay to disappoint people sometimes; you can't control their expectations.
AND, being disappointing doesn't make you a failure or unworthy of kindness.

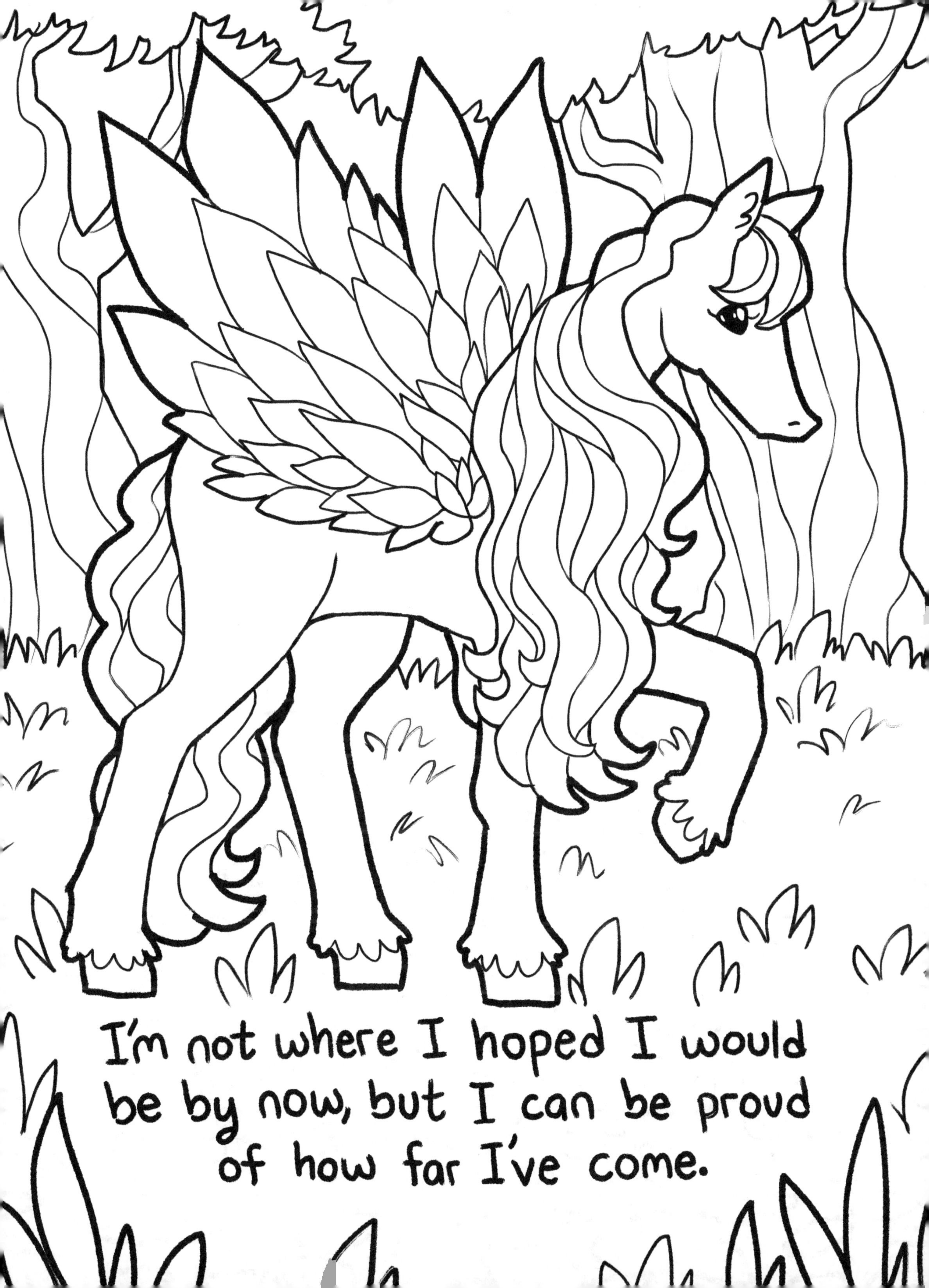
I'm not where I hoped I would
be by now, but I can be proud
of how far I've come.

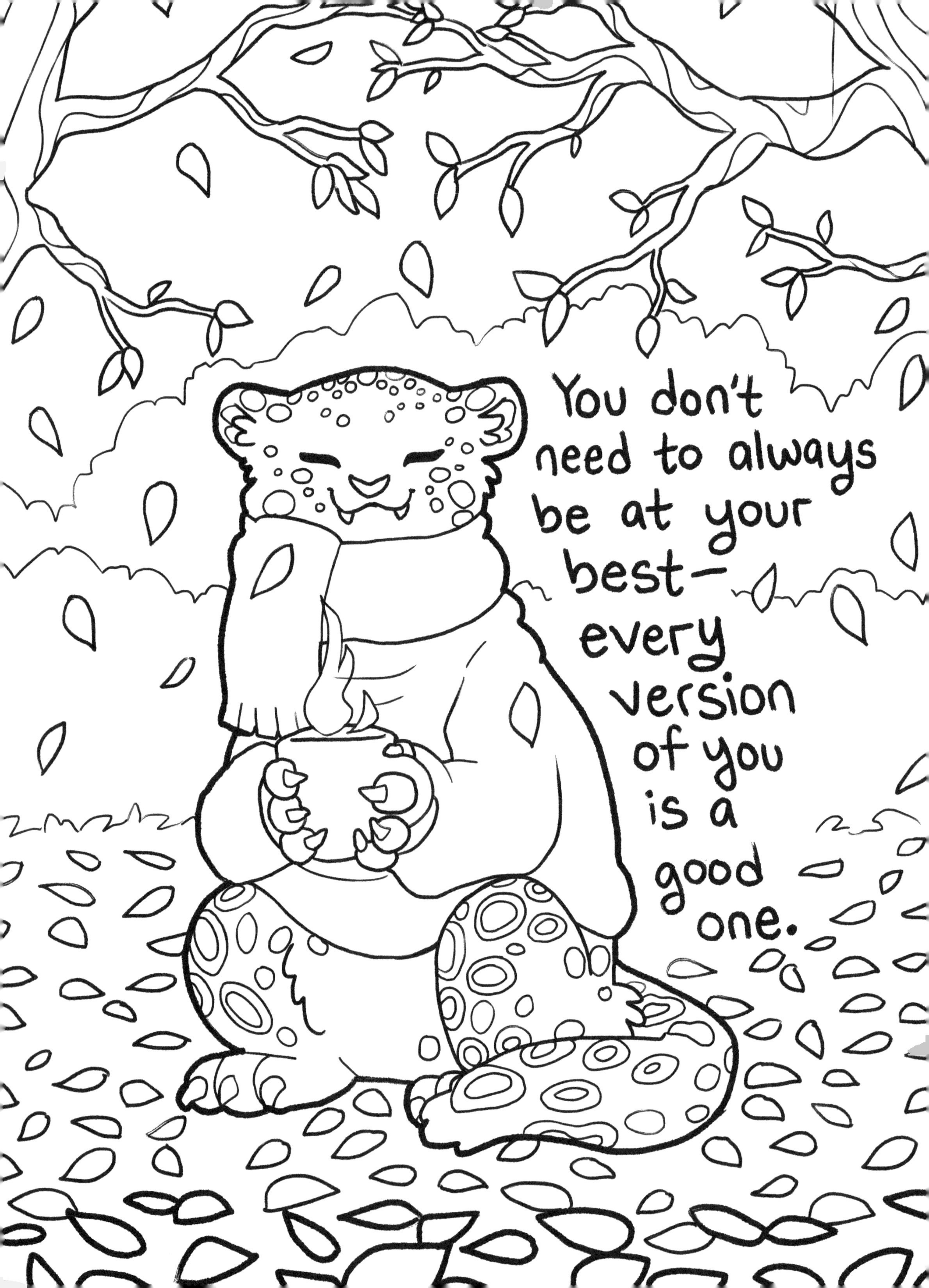
You don't need to always be at your best—every version of you is a good one.

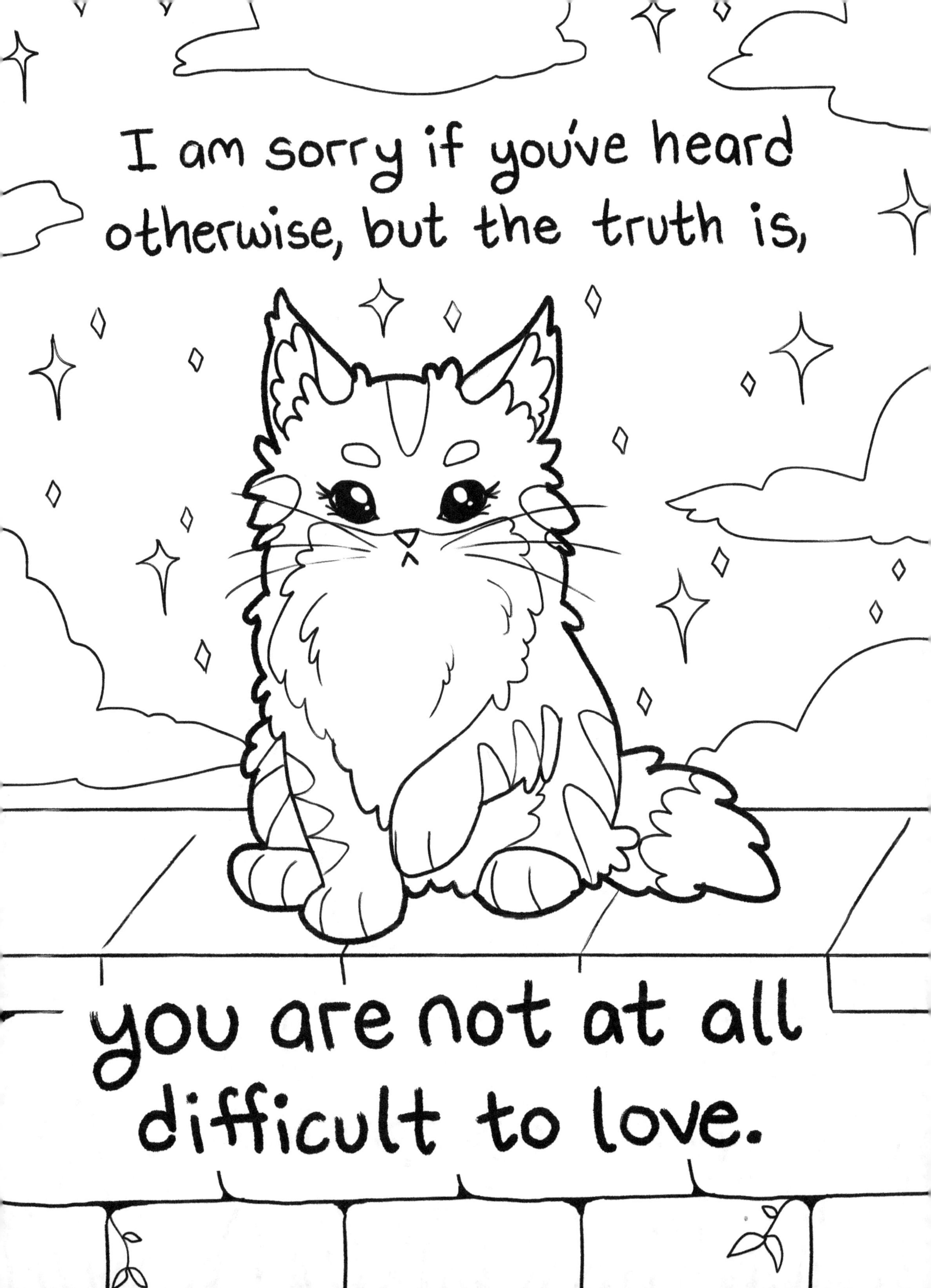
I am sorry if you've heard otherwise, but the truth is,
you are not at all difficult to love.

You can be grateful and depressed at the same time.

You are not a bad person for struggling to find joy in things right now.

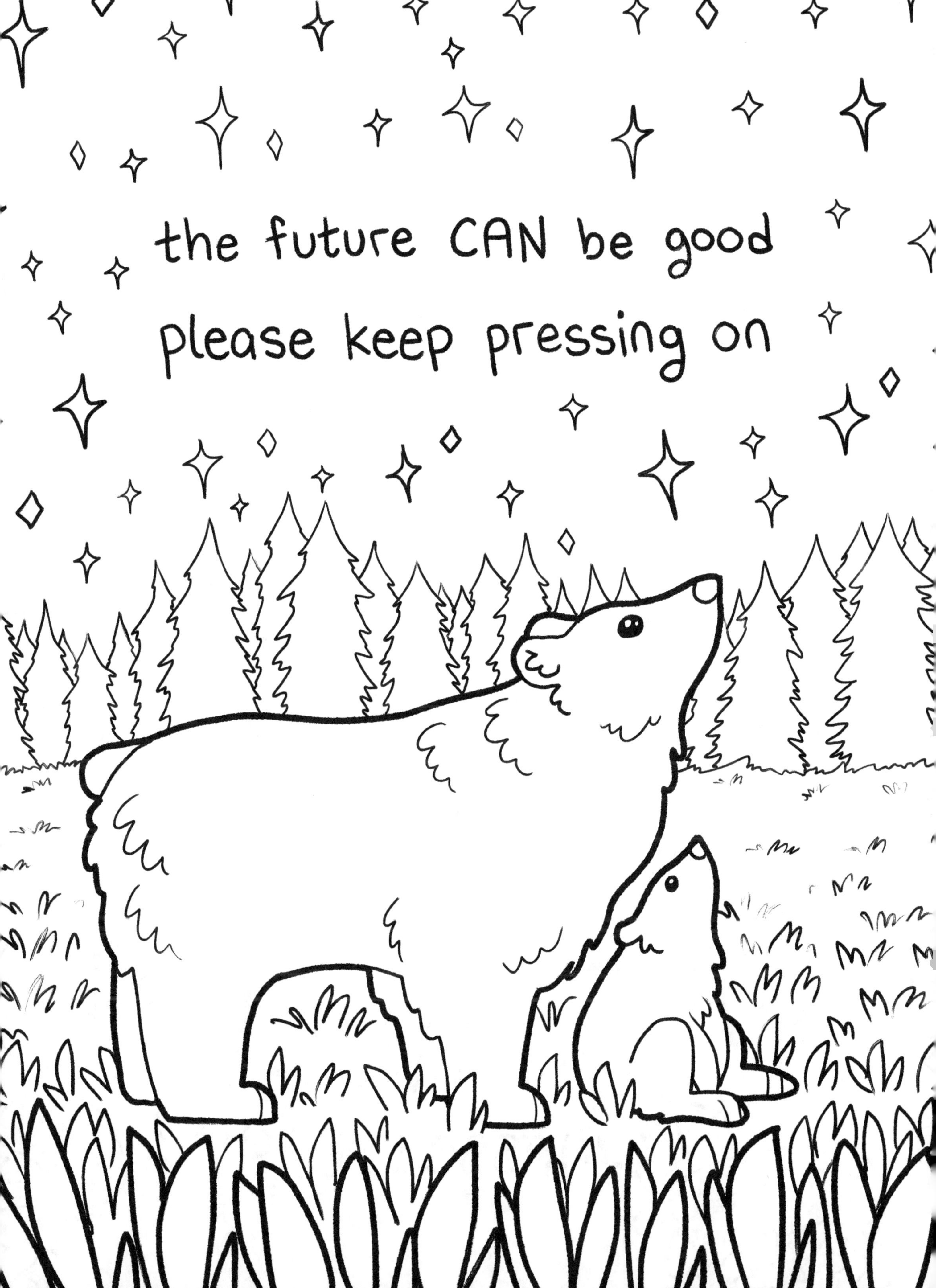
the future CAN be good
please keep pressing on

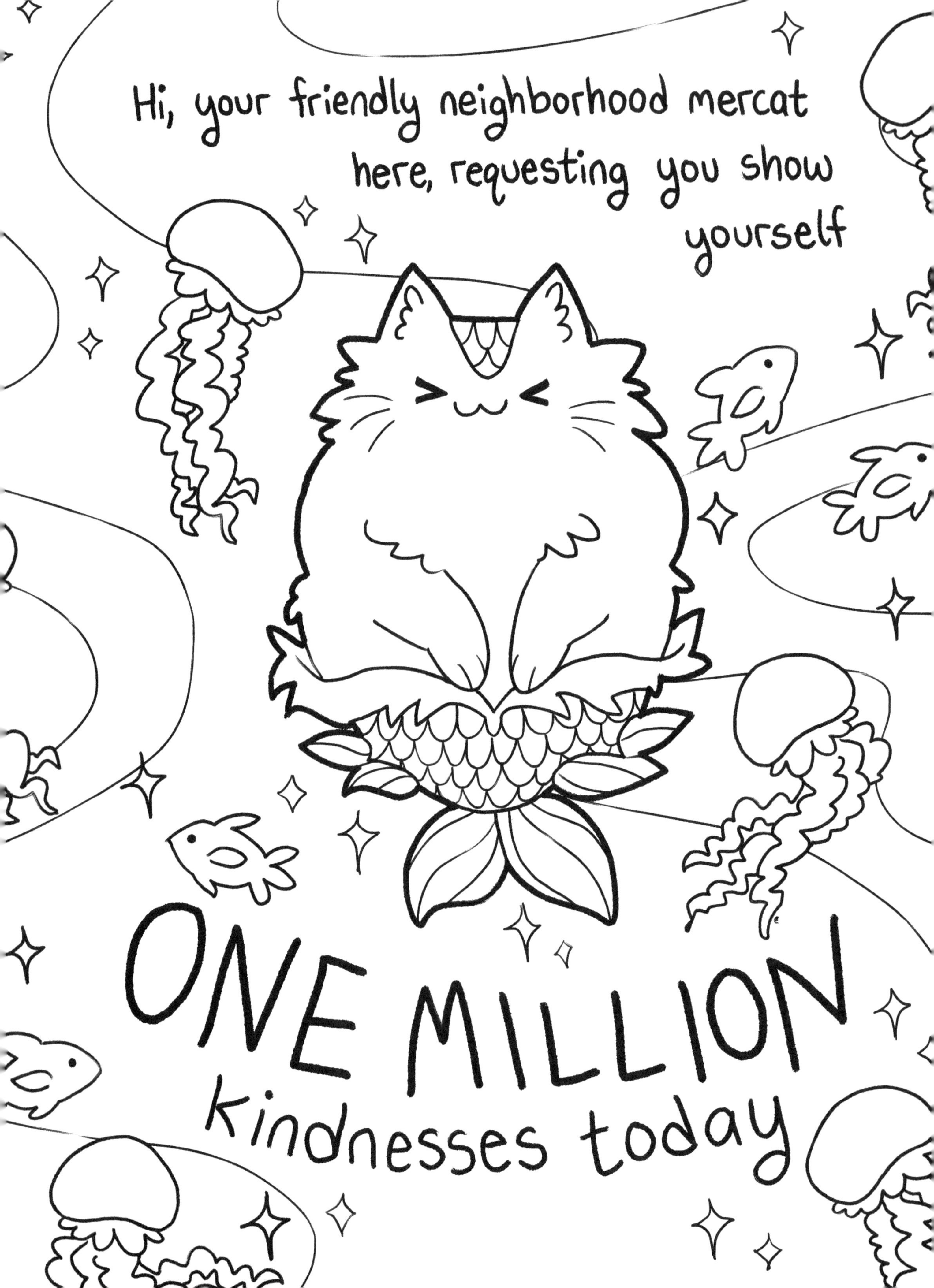
Hi, your friendly neighborhood mercat here, requesting you show yourself
ONE MILLION kindnesses today

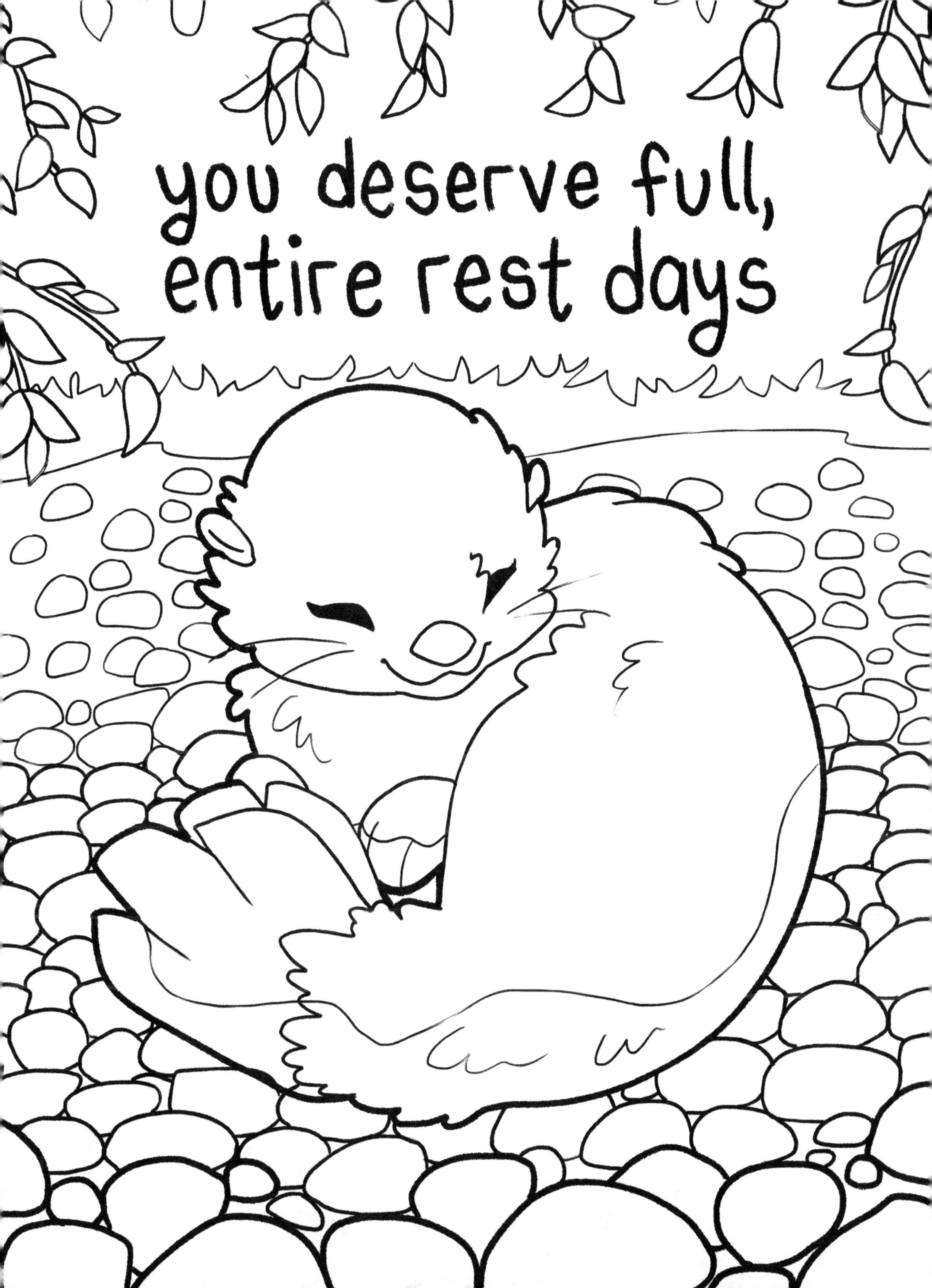
you deserve full,
entire rest days

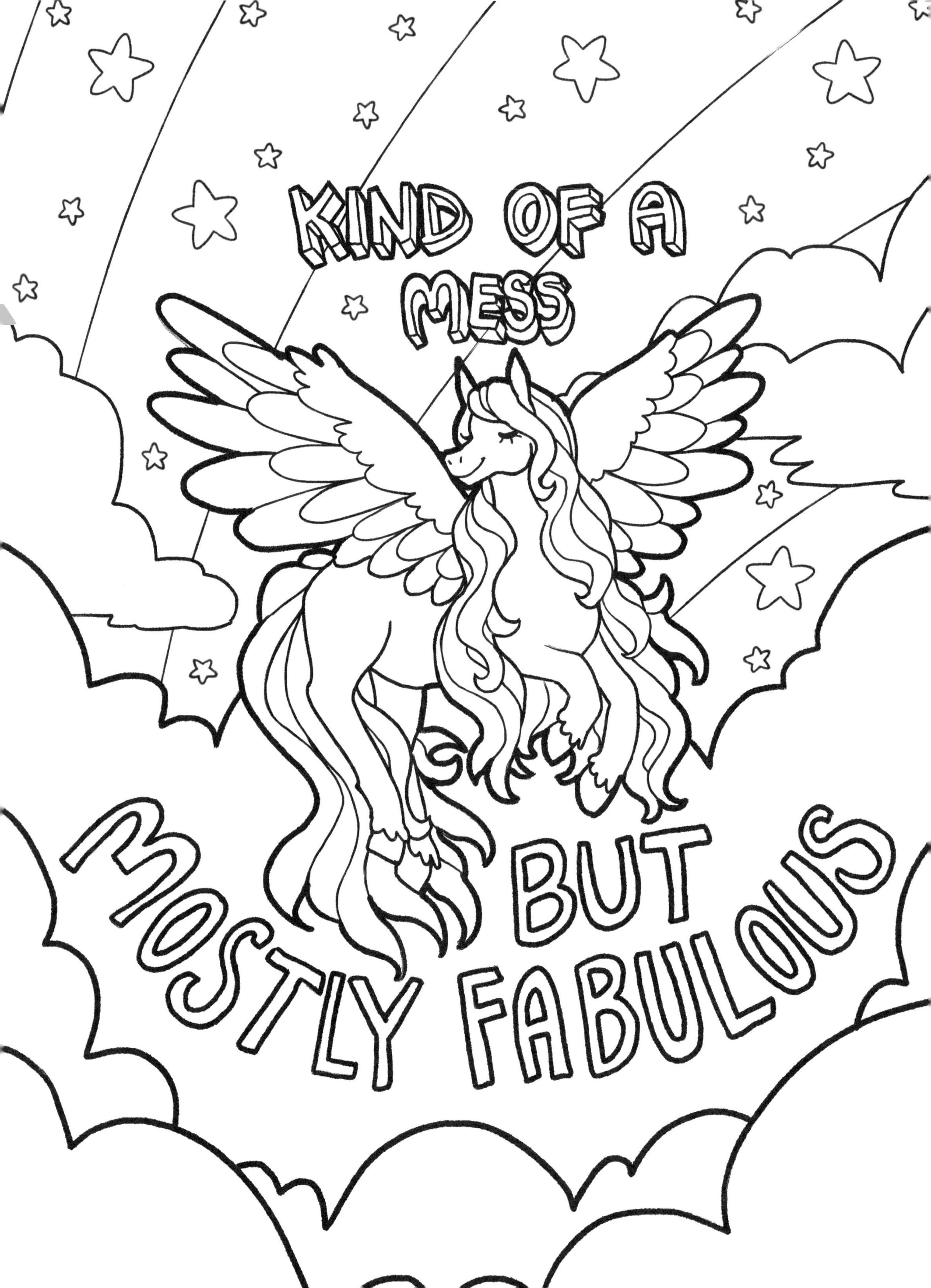
KIND OF A
MESS
BUT
MOSTLY FABULOUS

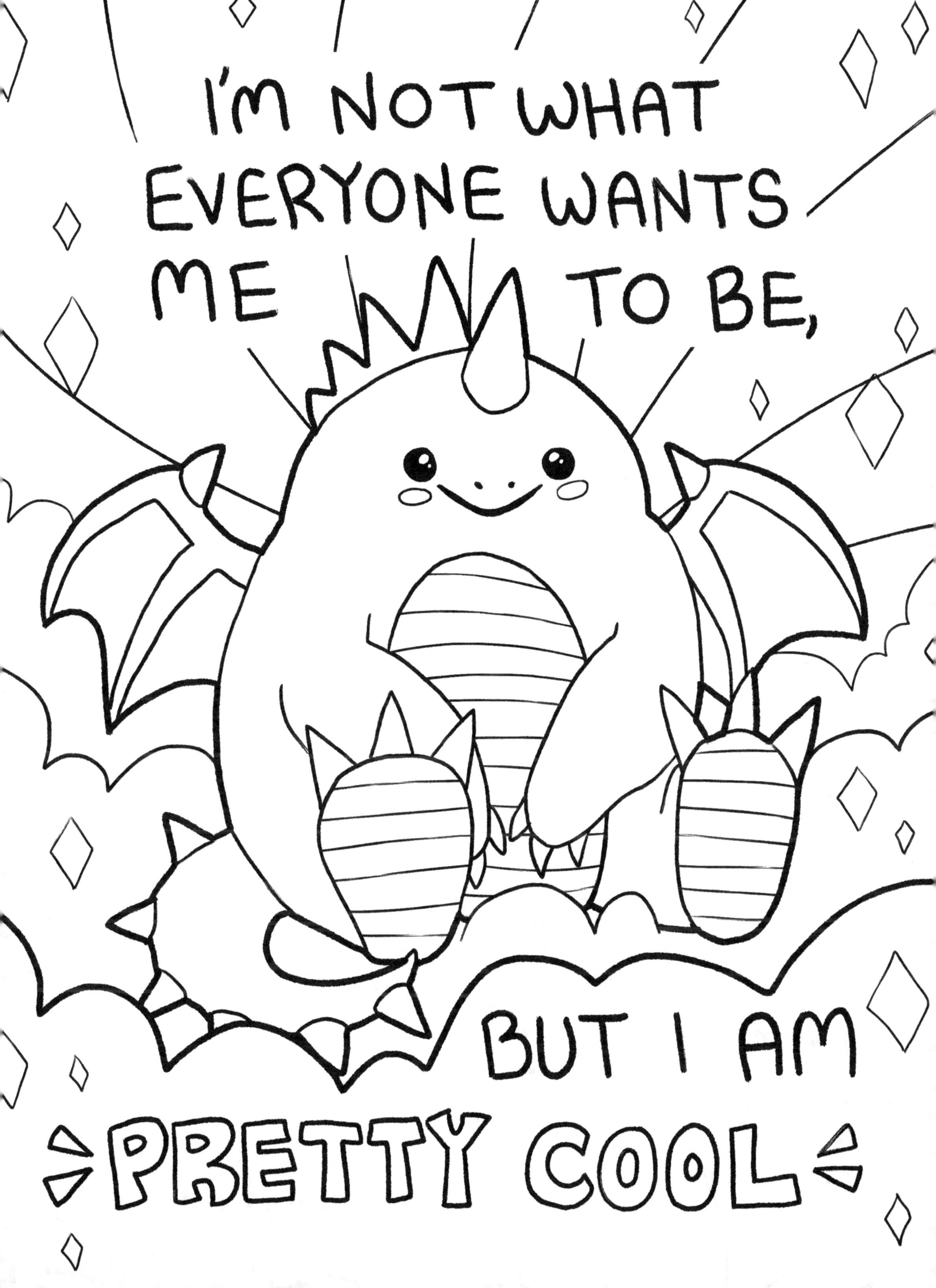
I'M NOT WHAT
EVERYONE WANTS
ME TO BE,
BUT I AM
PRETTY COOL

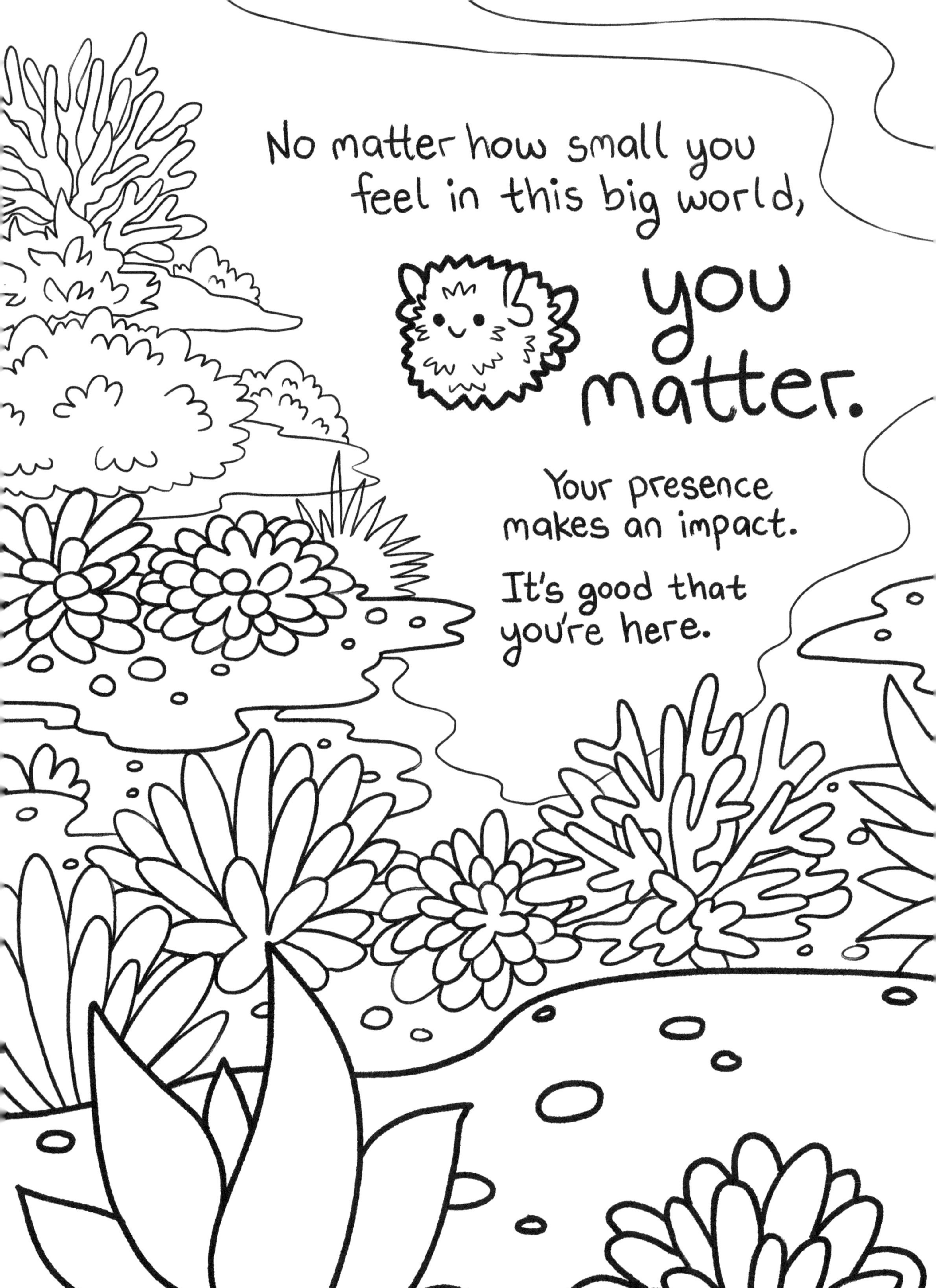
No matter how small you feel in this big world,
you matter.
Your presence makes an impact.
It's good that you're here.

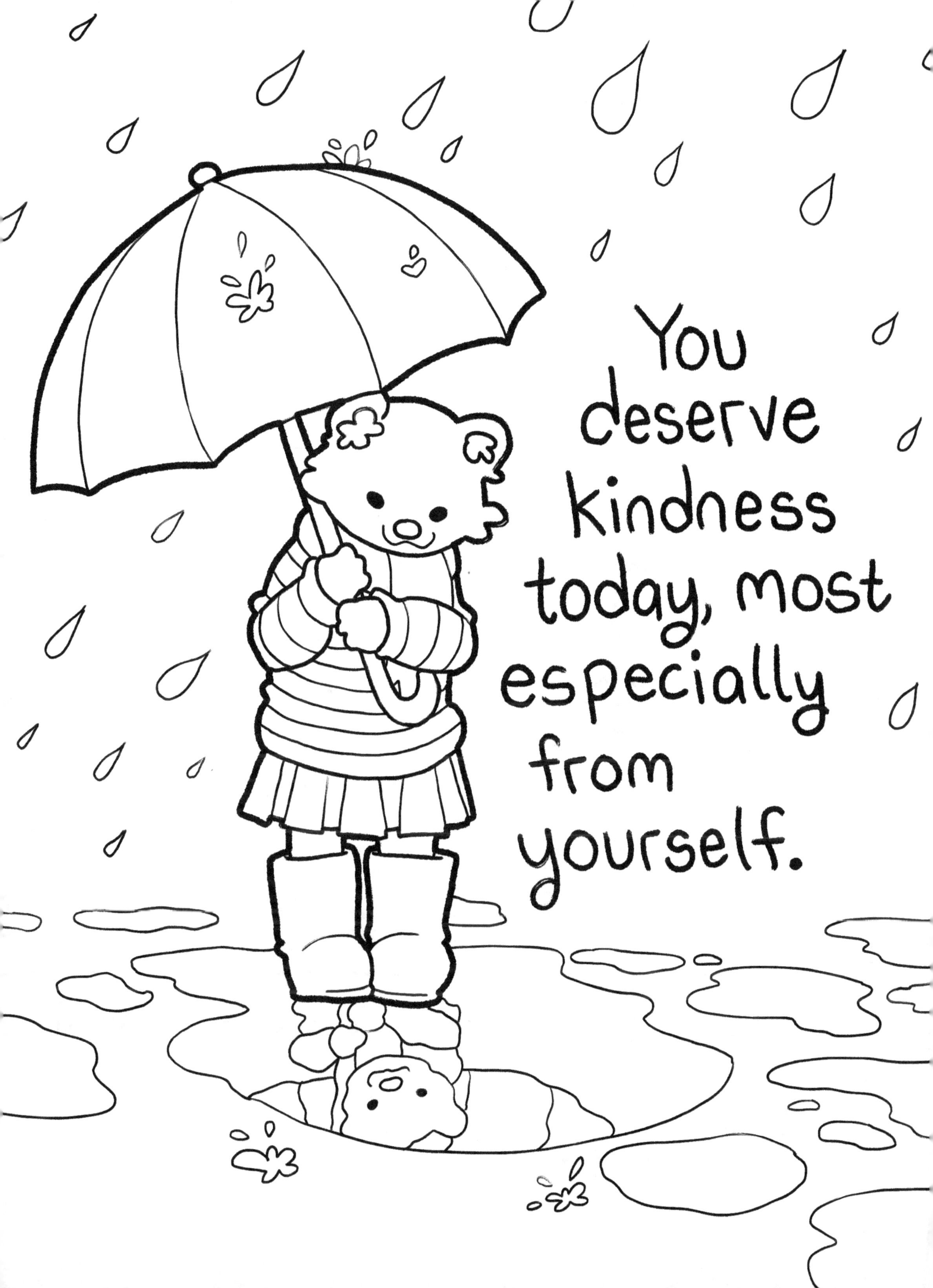
You deserve kindness today, most especially from yourself.

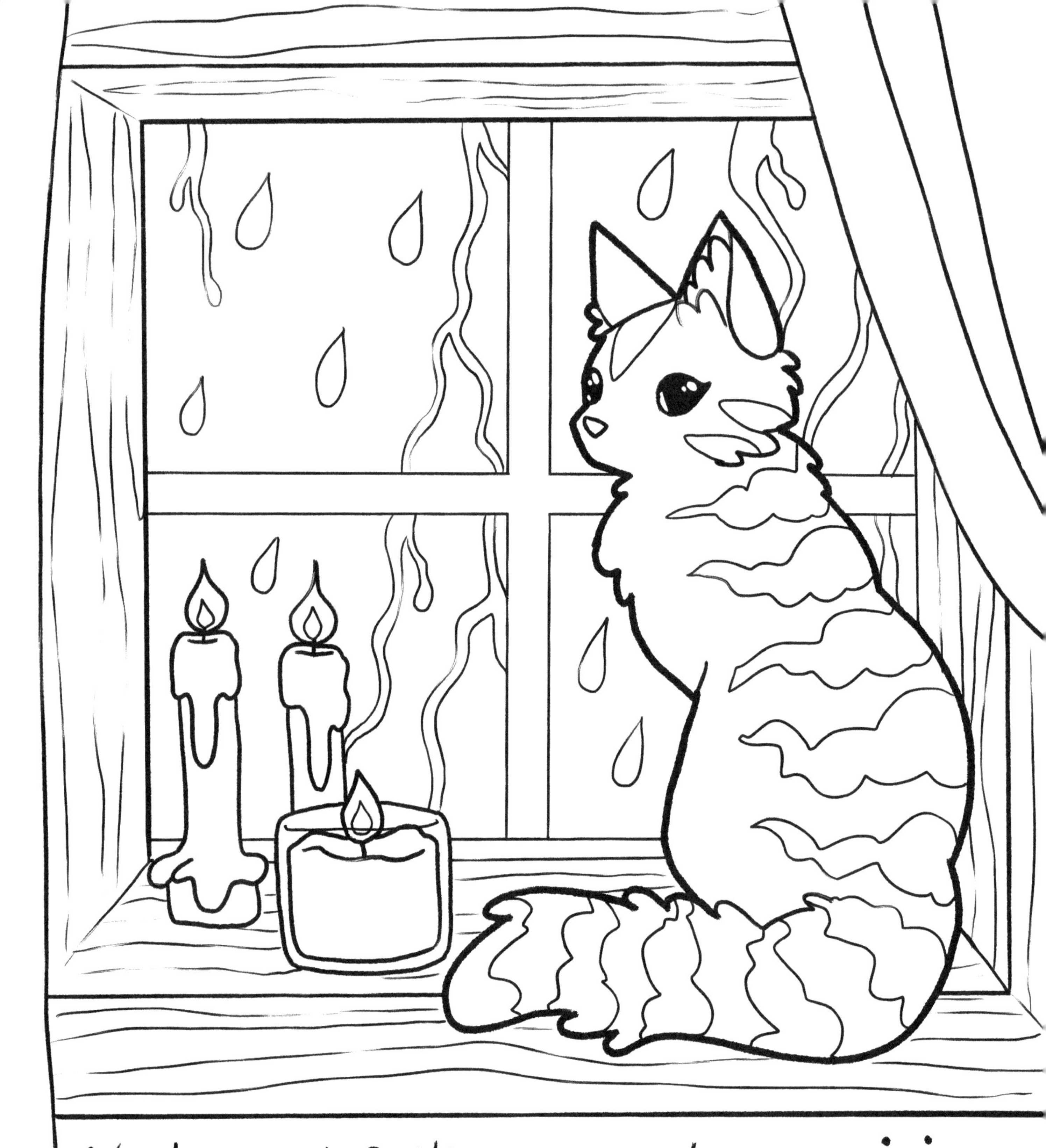

You're not failing— you're surviving difficult times. Struggles are to be expected.

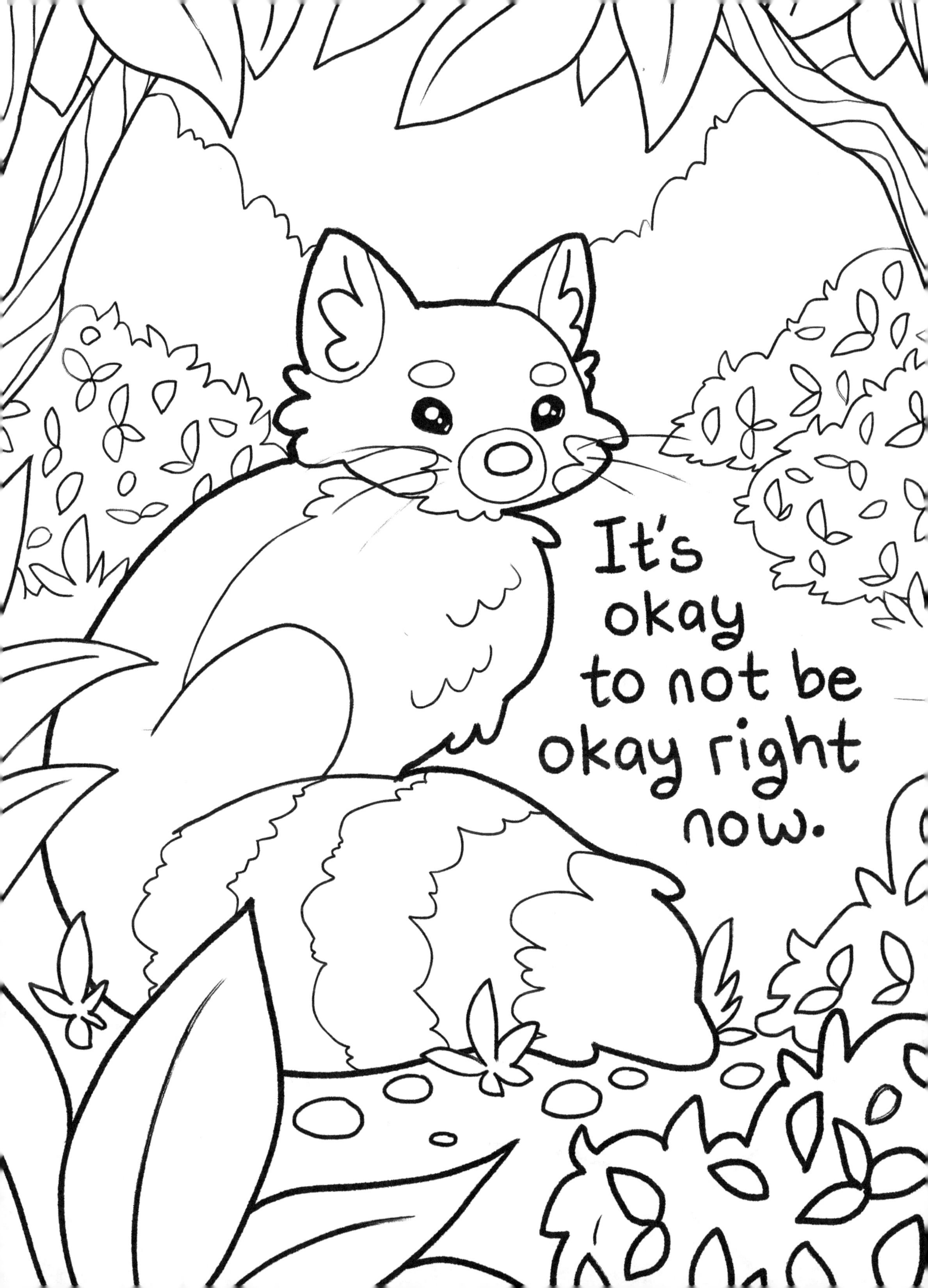
It's
okay
to not be
okay right
now.

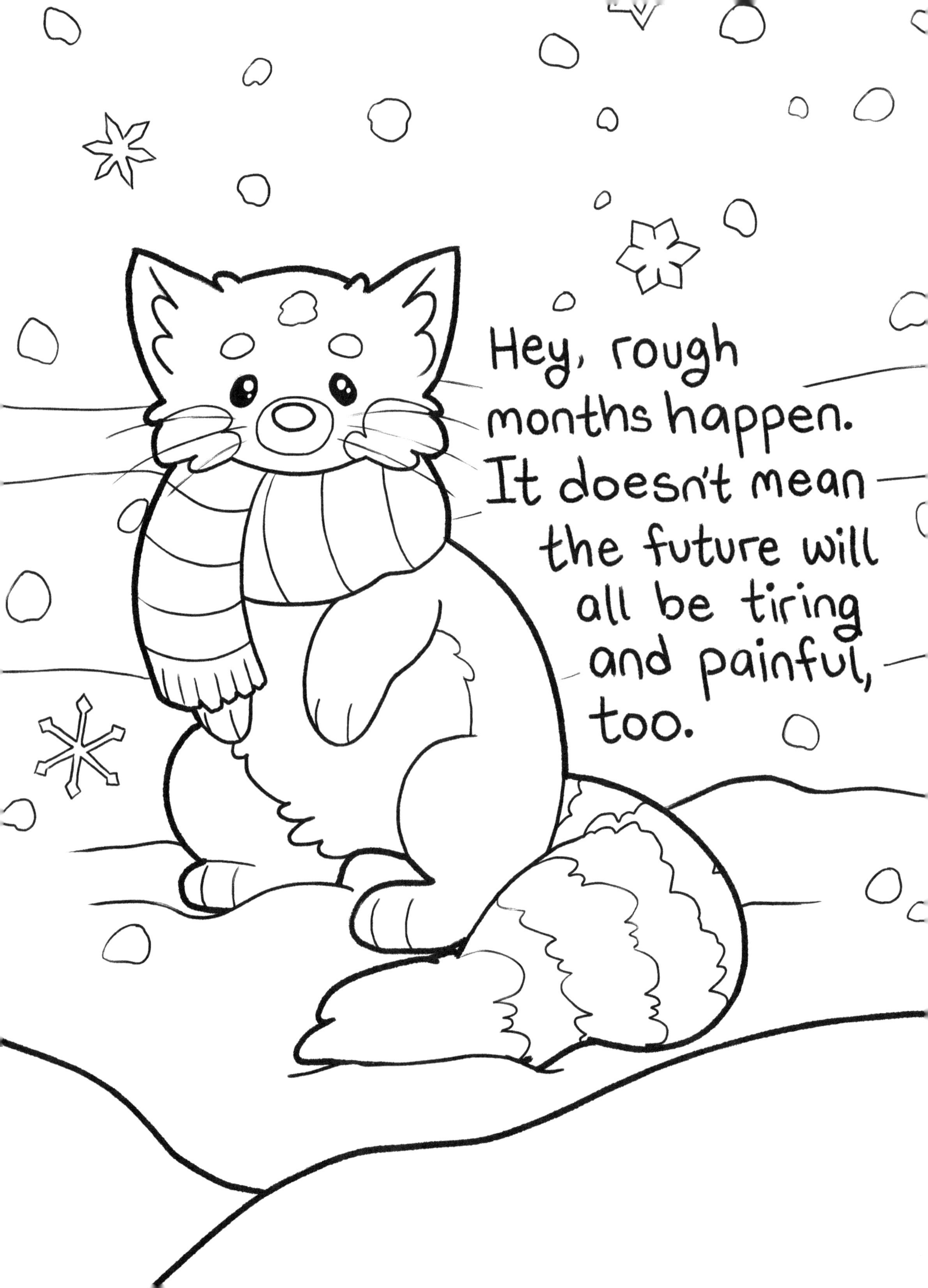
Hey, rough months happen. It doesn't mean the future will all be tiring and painful, too.

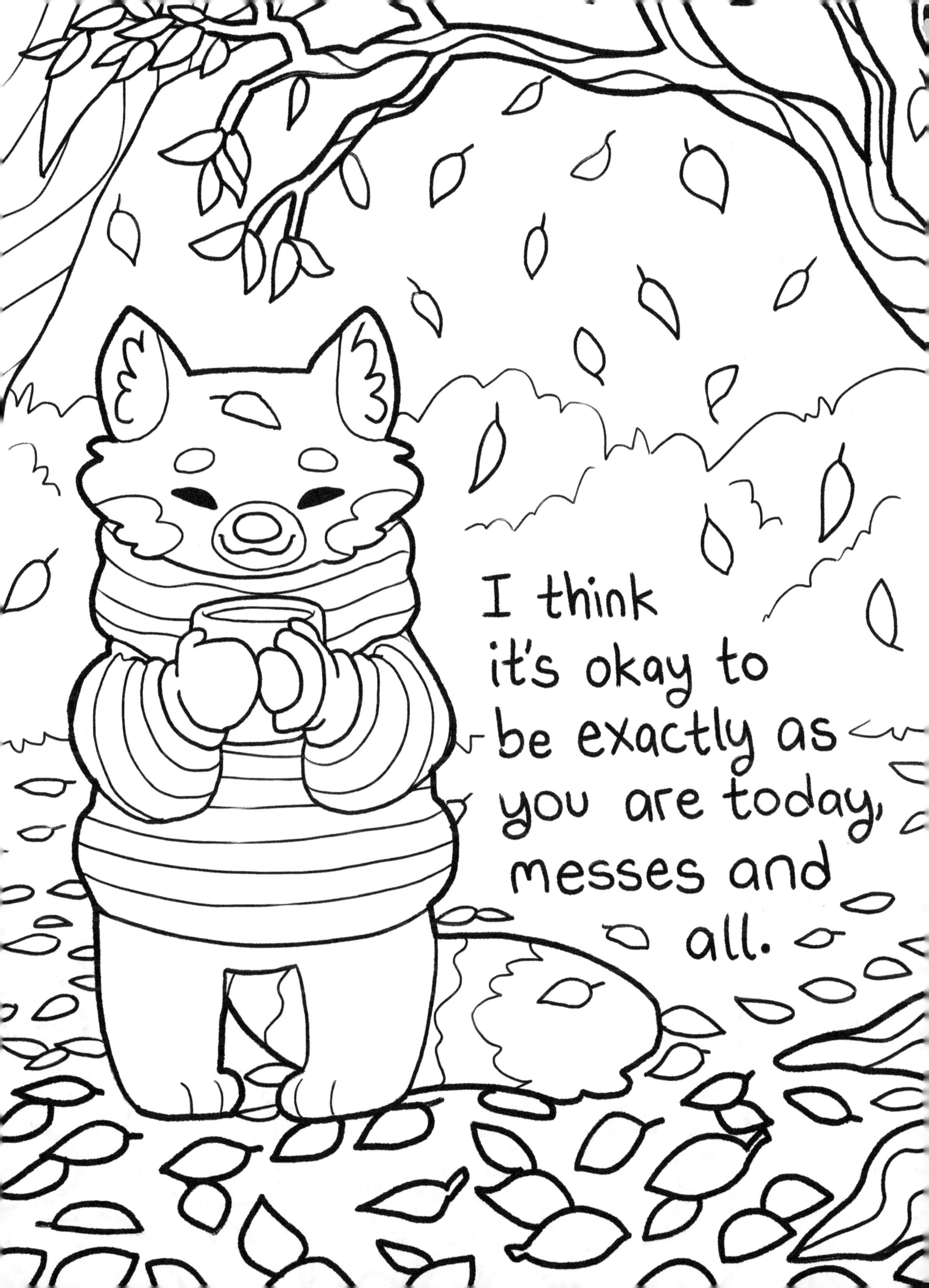
I think
it's okay to
be exactly as
you are today,
messes and
all.

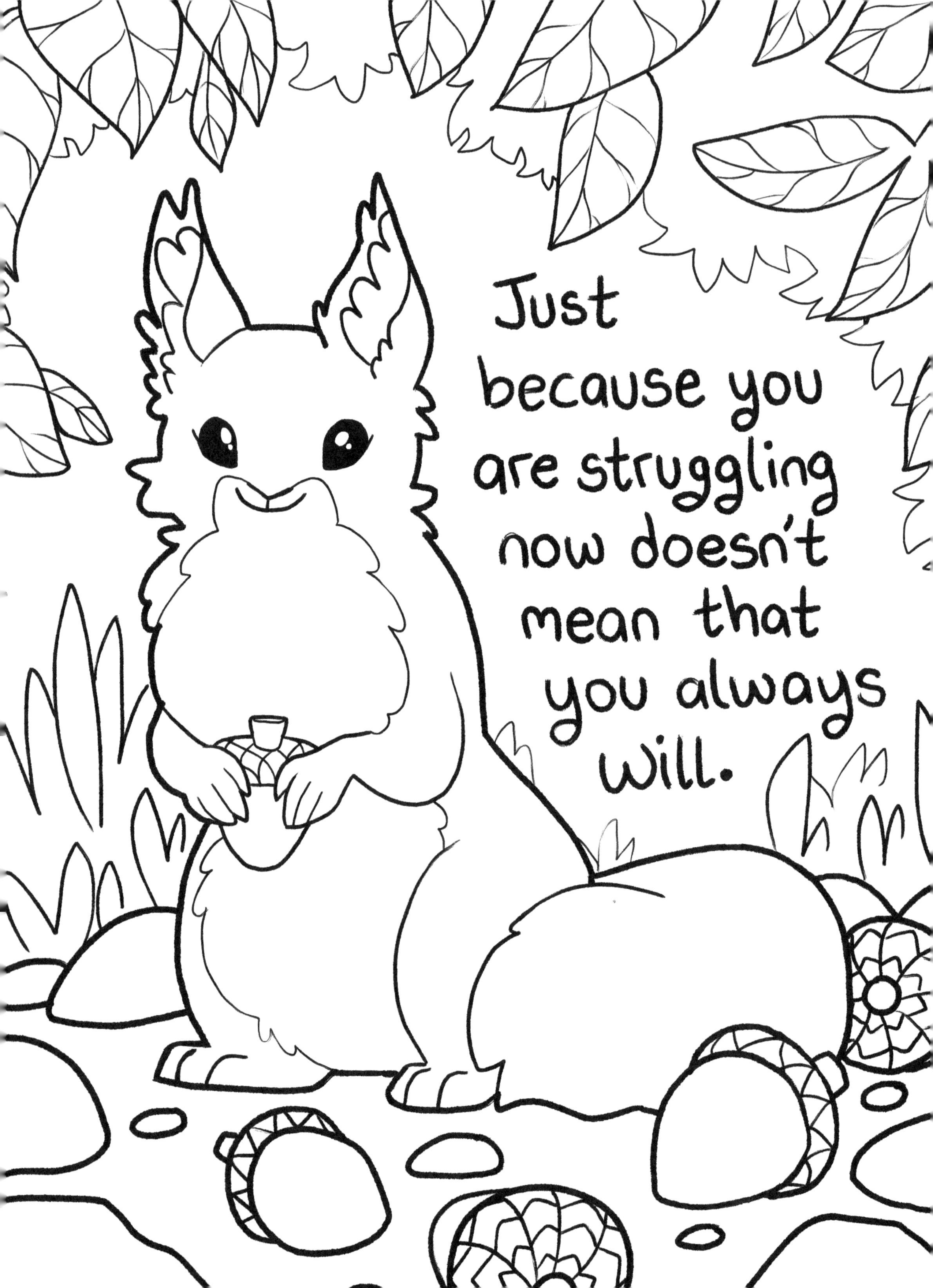
Just
because you
are struggling
now doesn't
mean that
you always
will.

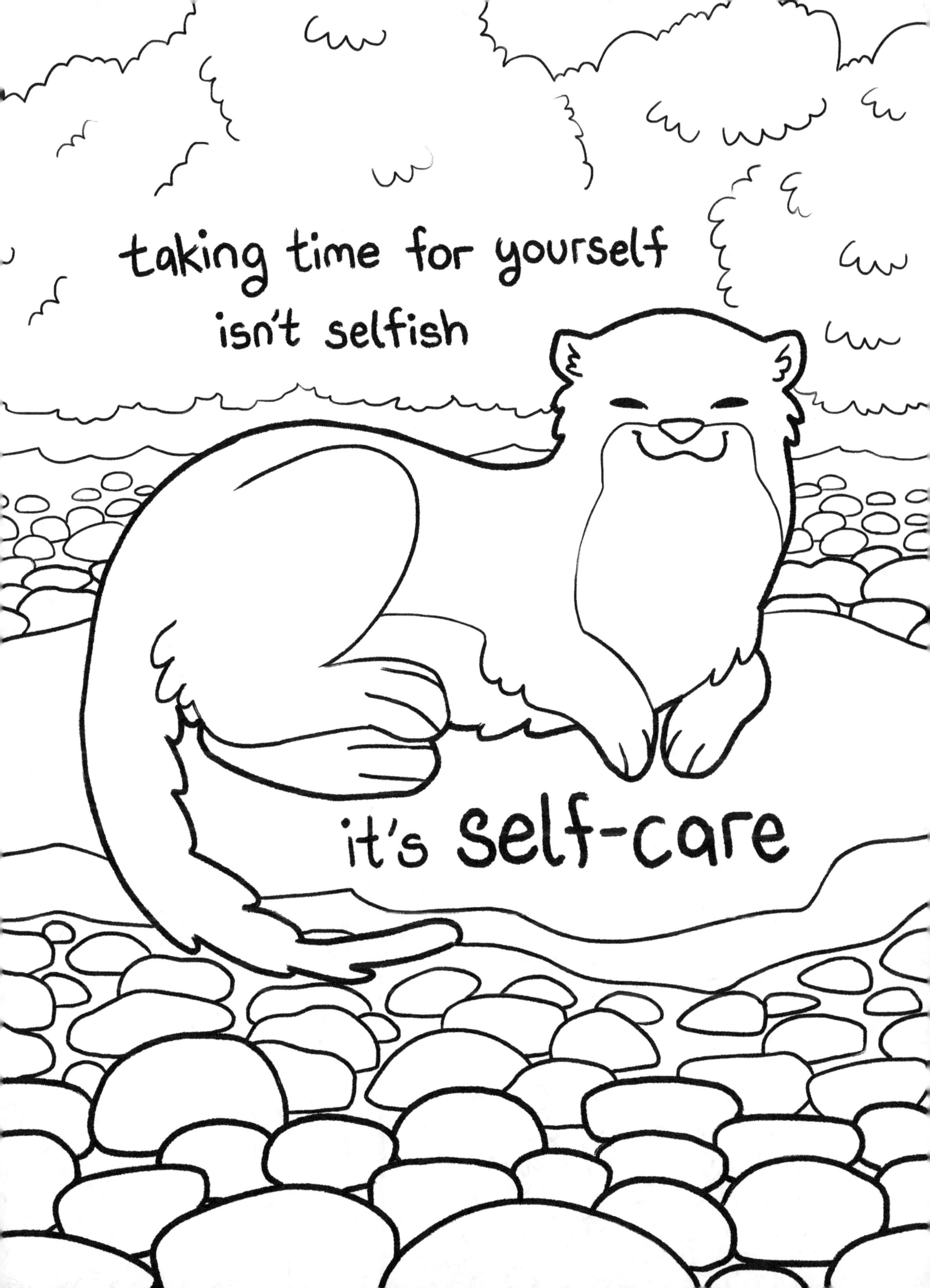
taking time for yourself
isn't selfish
it's self-care

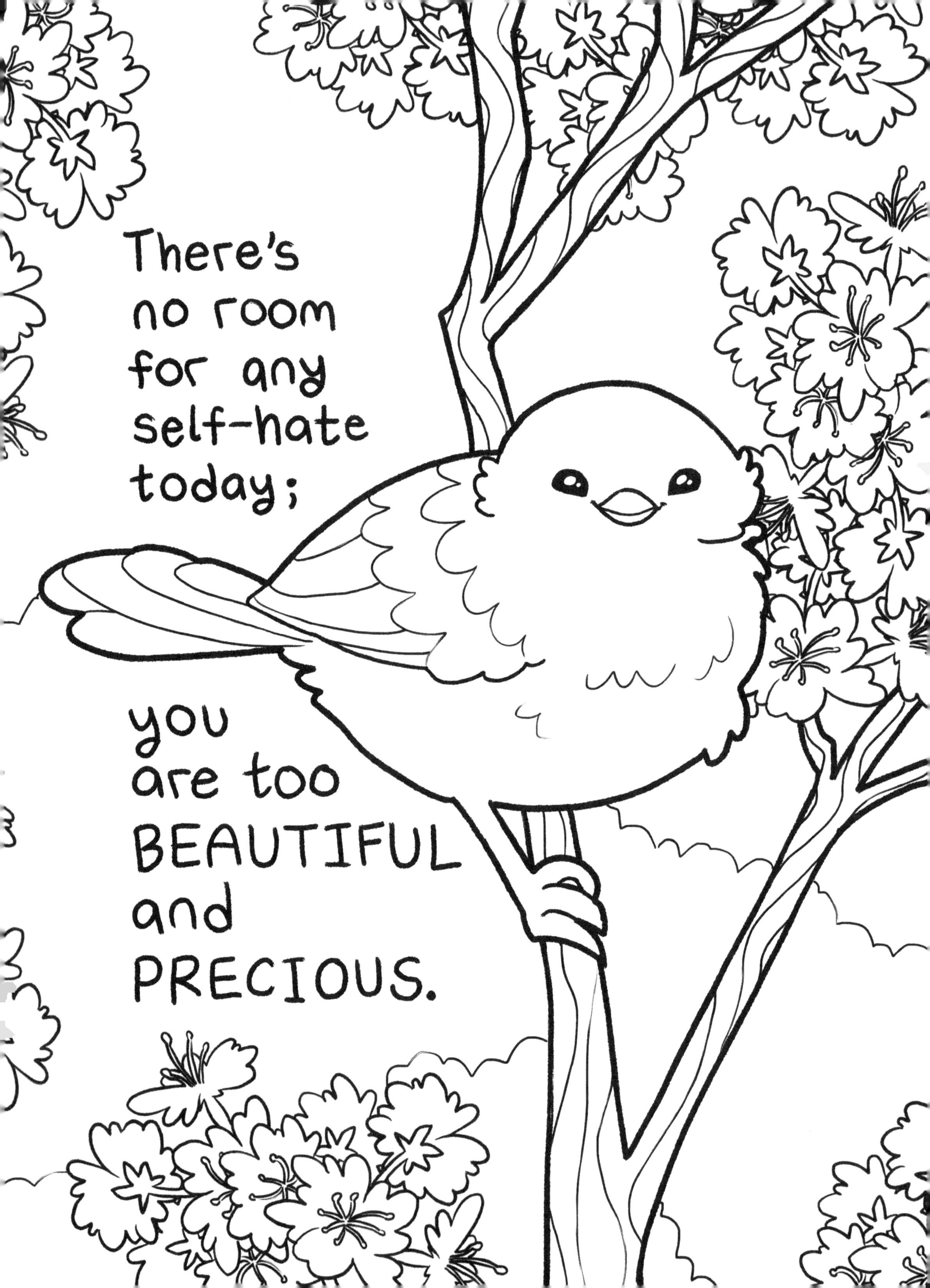
There's
no room
for any
self-hate
today;
you
are too
BEAUTIFUL
and
PRECIOUS.

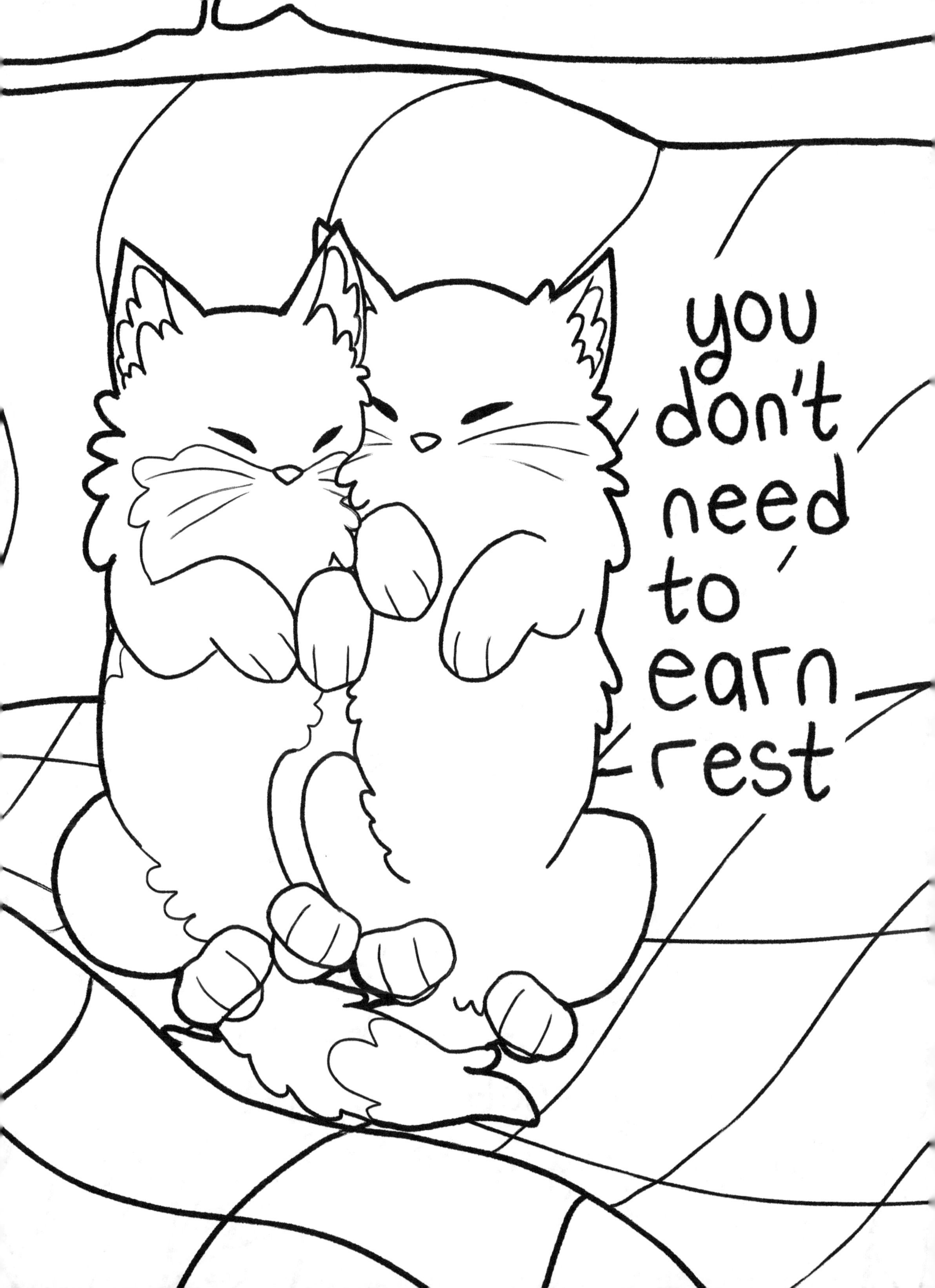
you don't need to earn rest

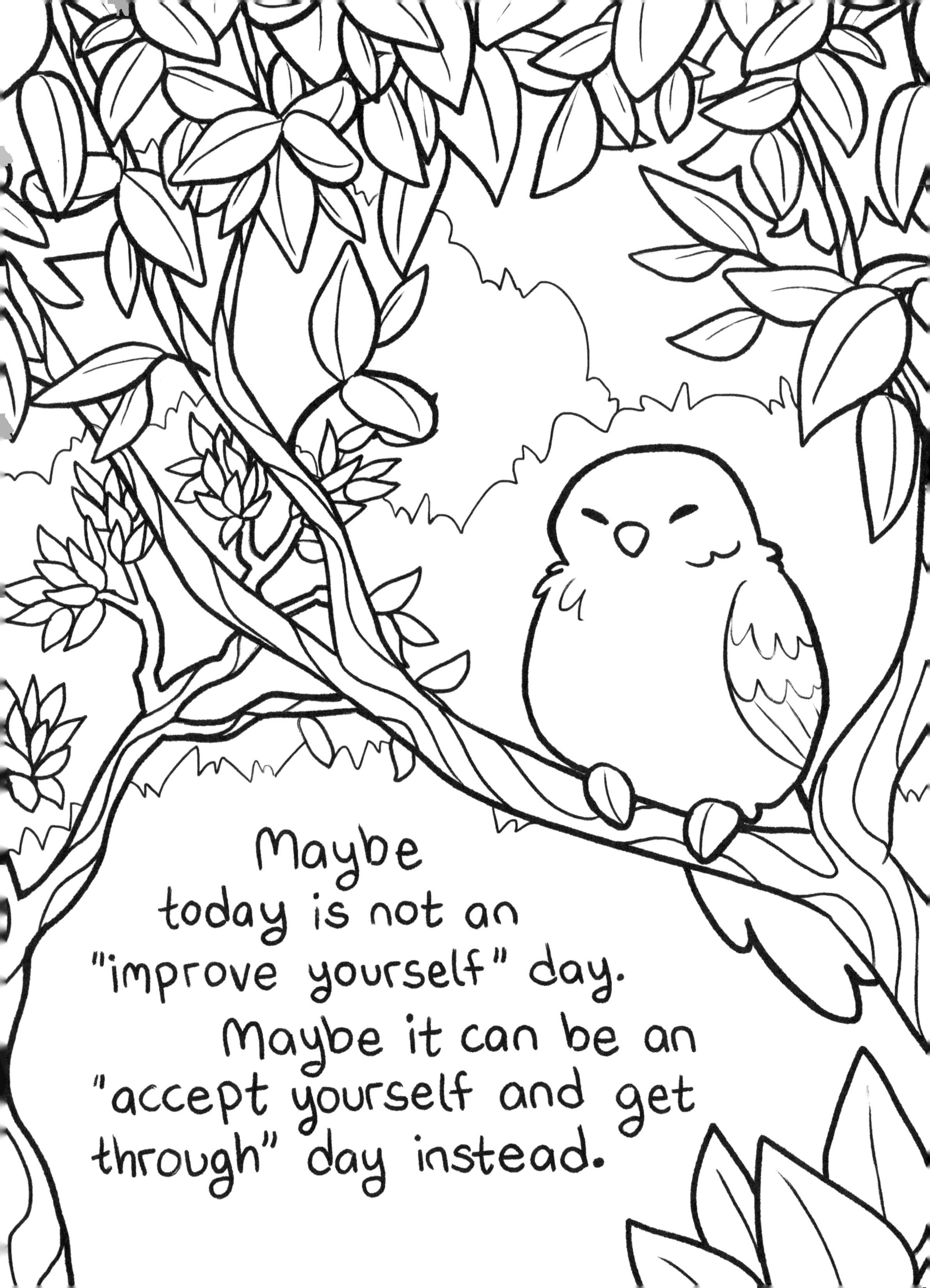
Maybe
today is not an
"improve yourself" day.
Maybe it can be an
"accept yourself and get
through" day instead.

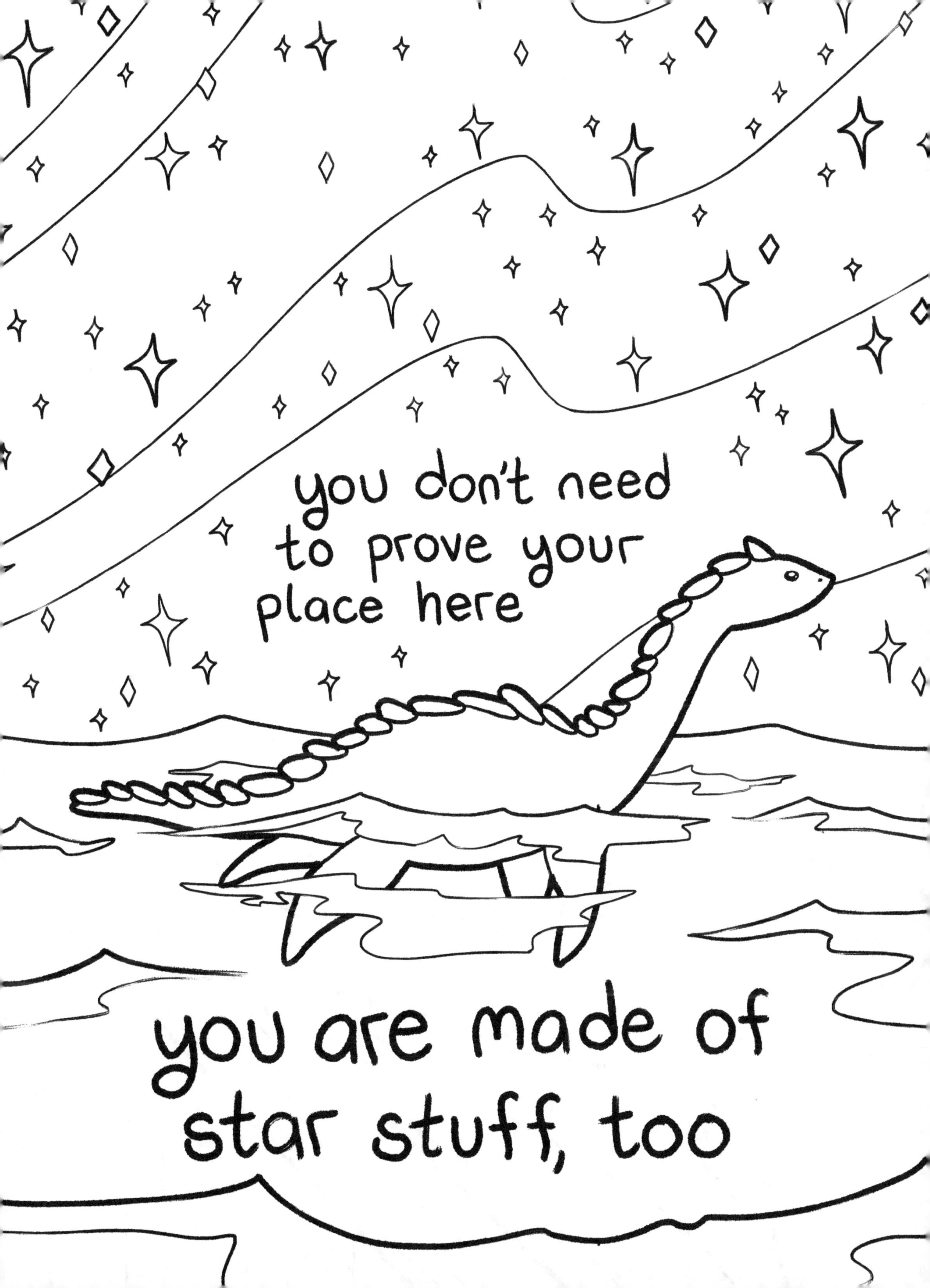
you don't need
to prove your
place here
you are made of
star stuff, too

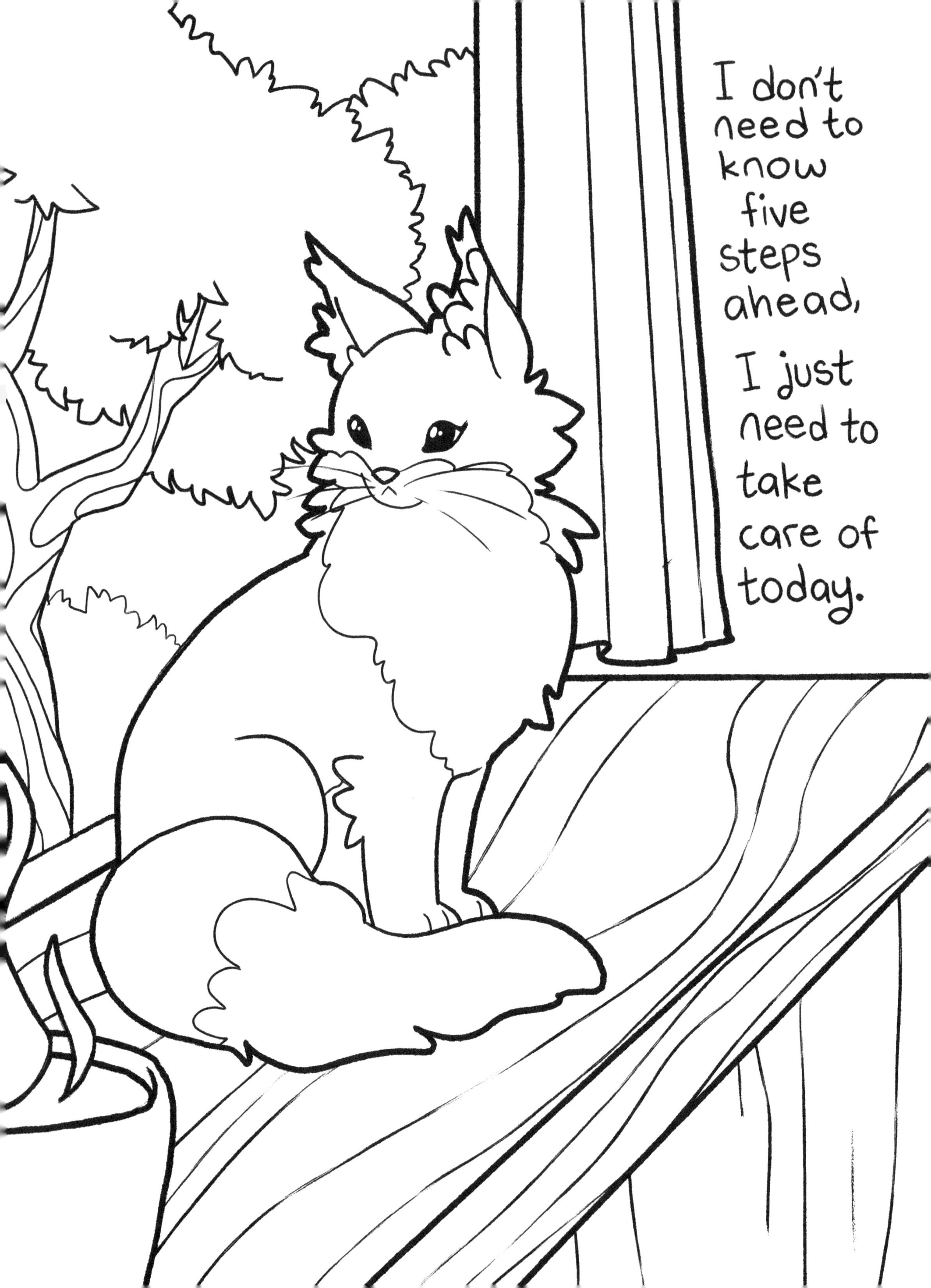
I don't need to know five steps ahead,
I just need to take care of today.

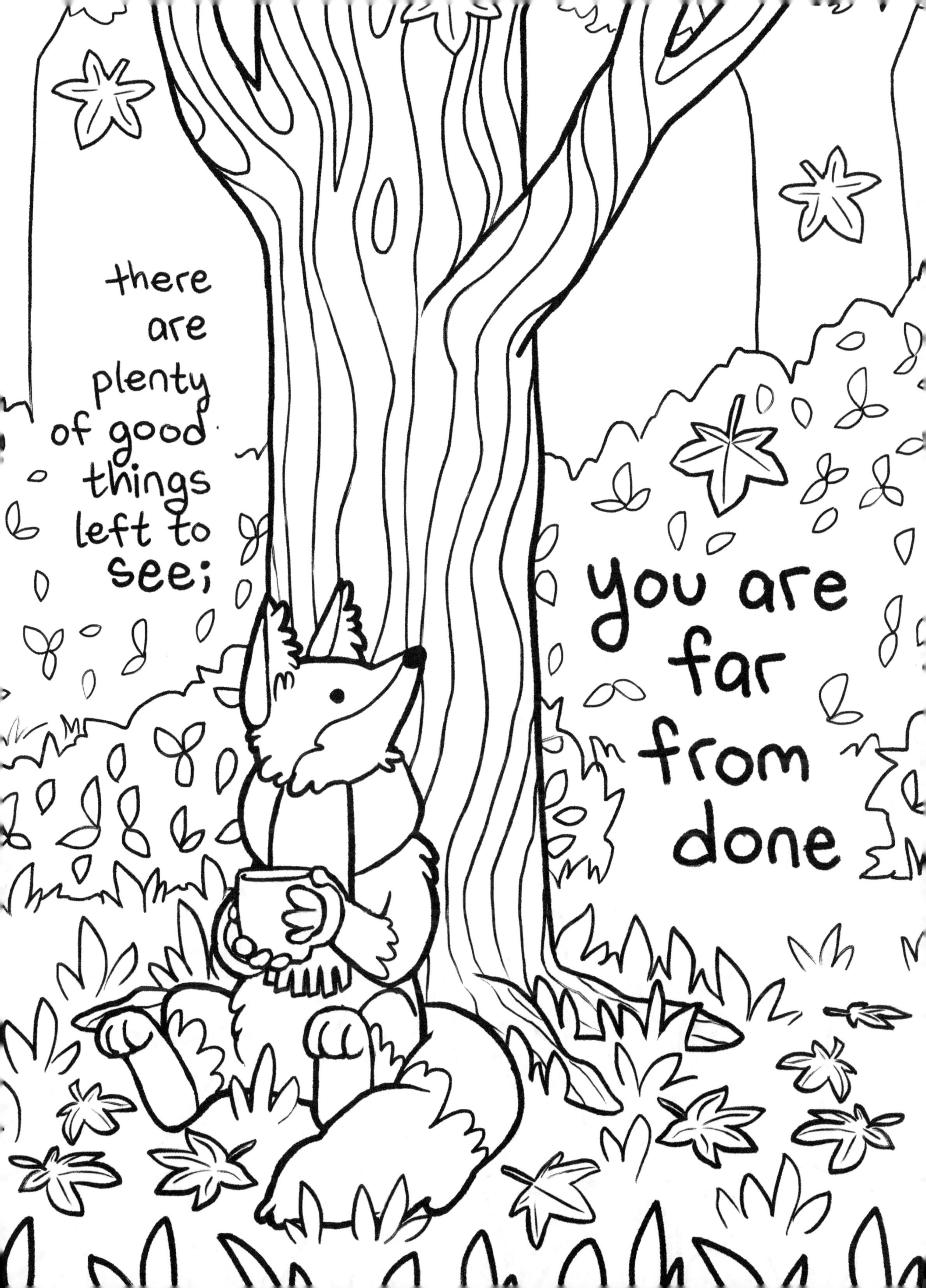
there are plenty of good things left to see;
you are far from done

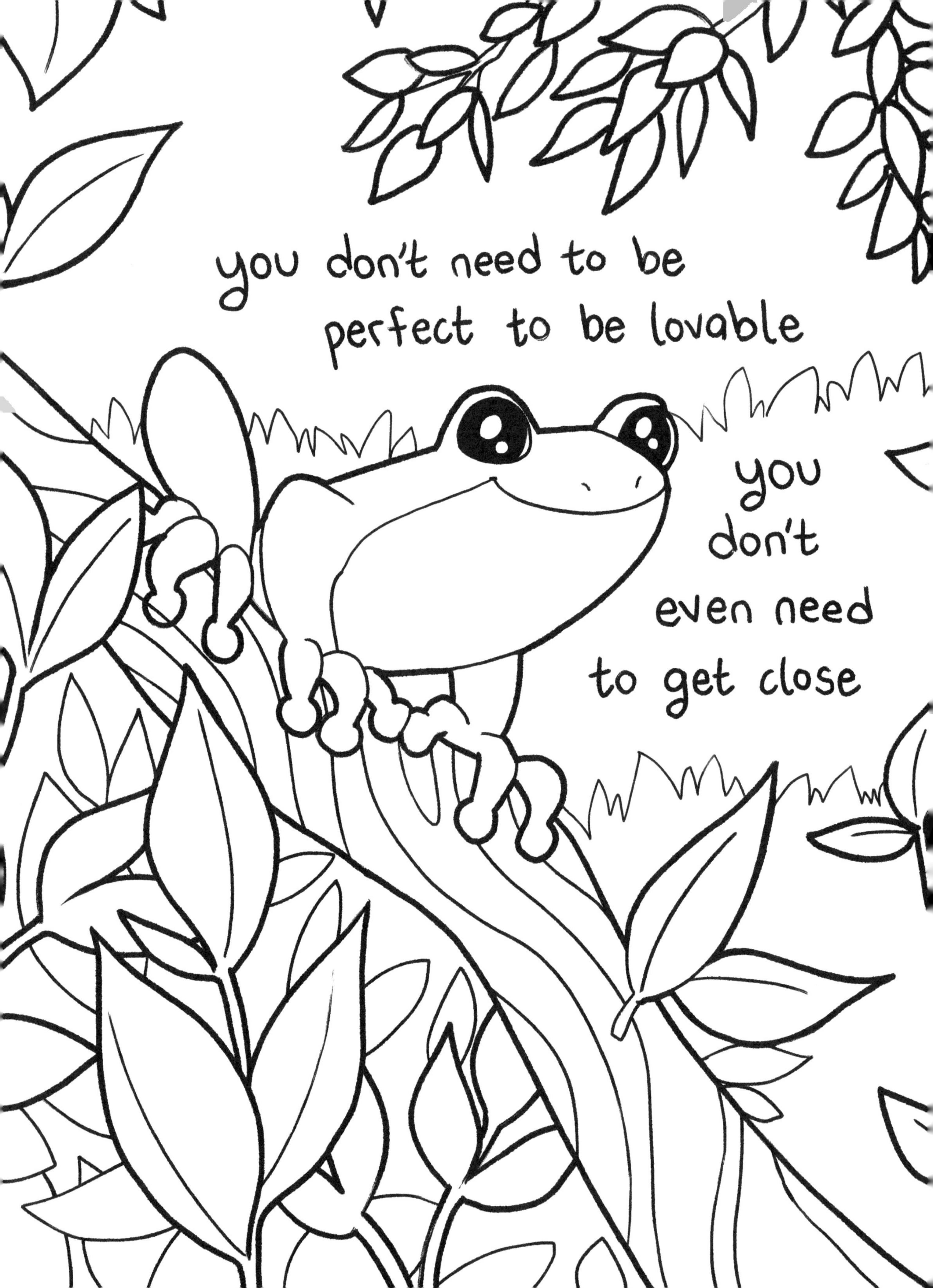
you don't need to be
perfect to be lovable
you
don't
even need
to get close

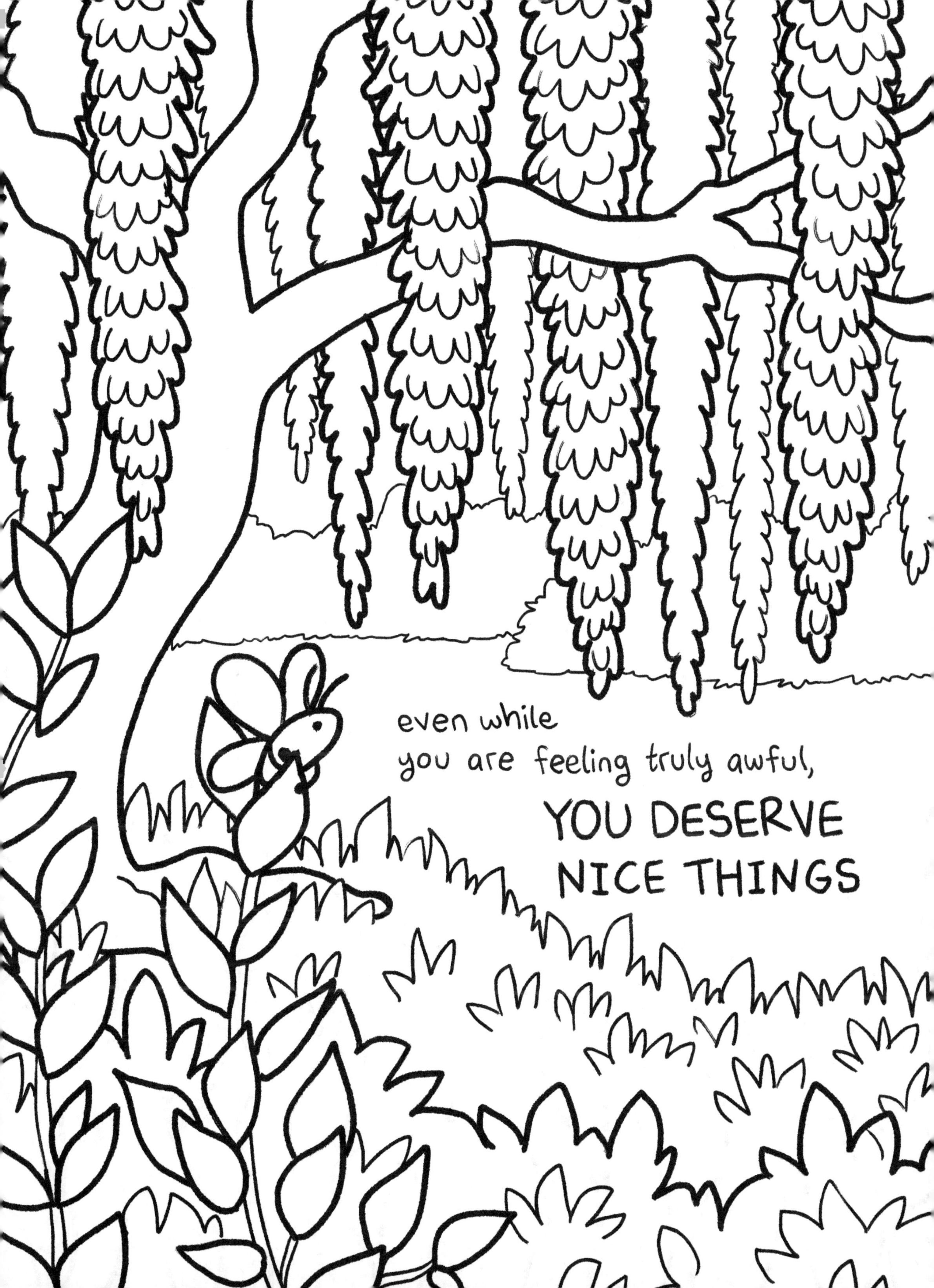
even while
you are feeling truly awful,
YOU DESERVE
NICE THINGS

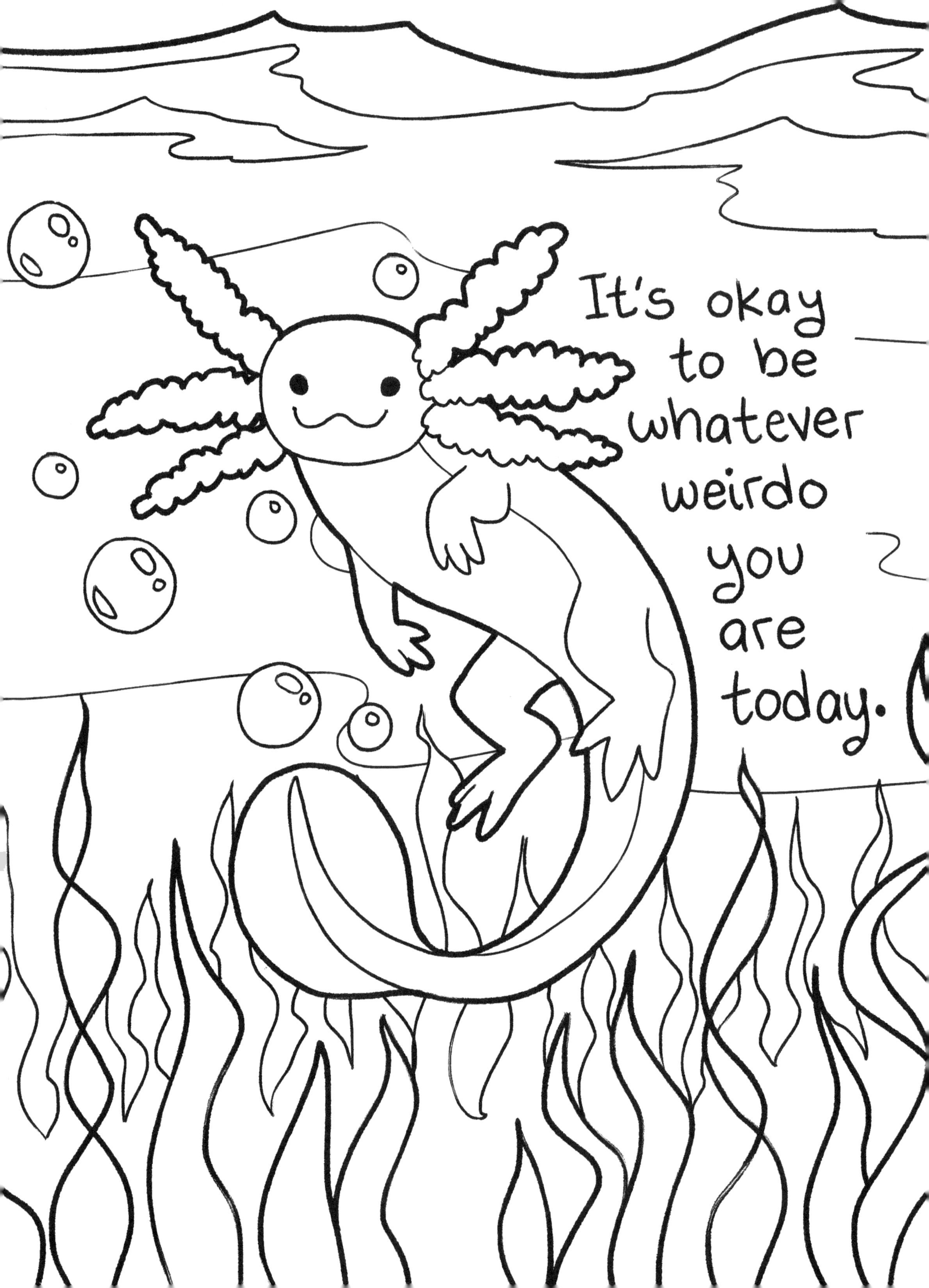
It's okay
to be
whatever
weirdo
you
are
today.

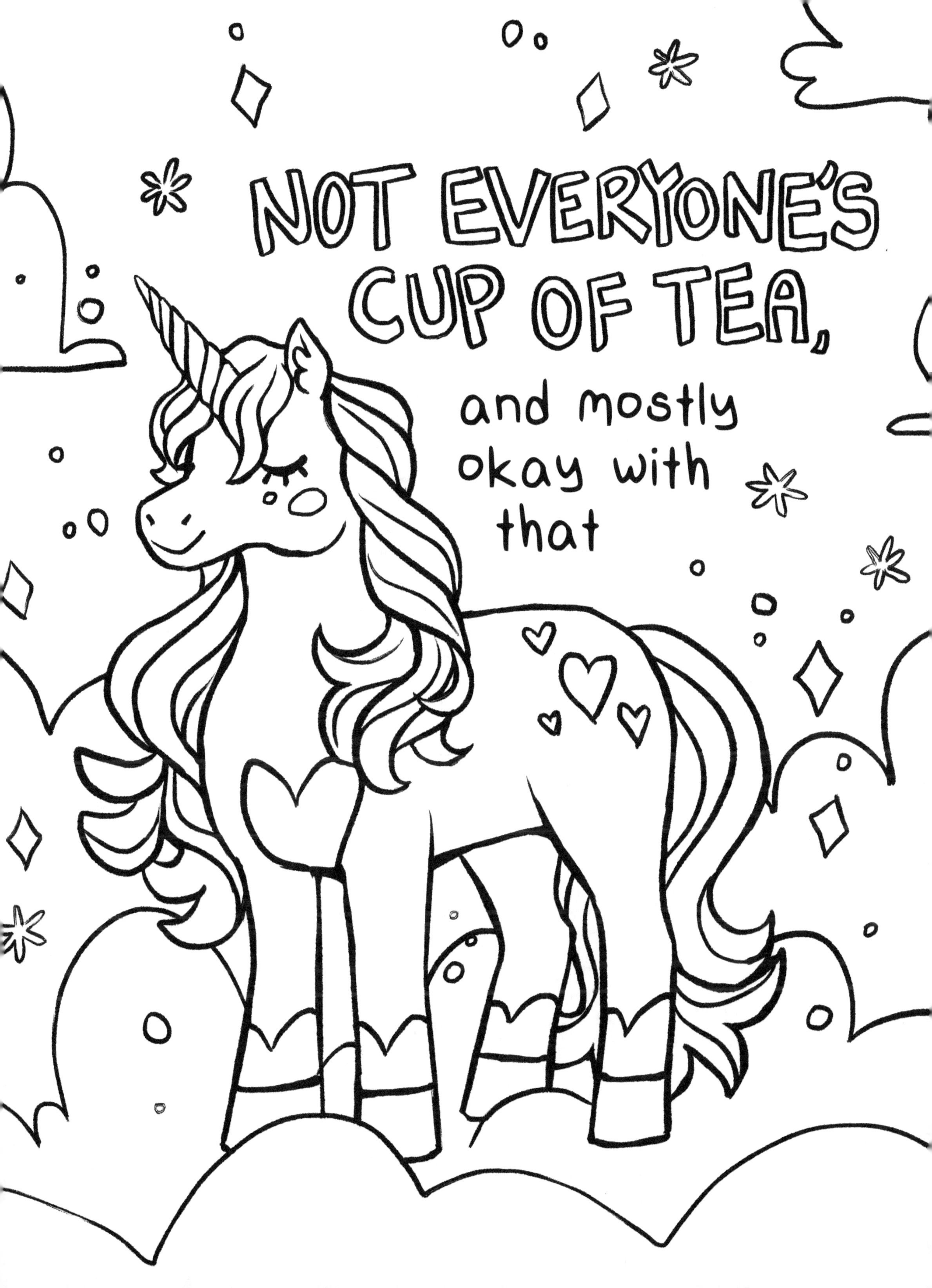
NOT EVERYONE'S
CUP OF TEA,
and mostly
okay with
that

About the Author

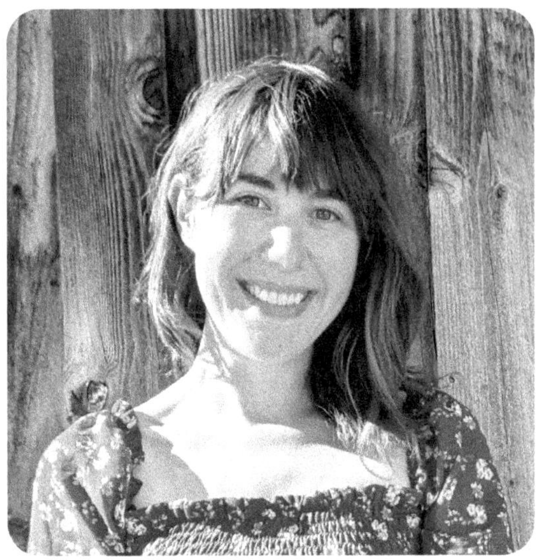

Kate Allan is an author, an artist, and the creator of the mental health art blog, *The Latest Kate*. She draws and writes with gentle comfort and encouragement about the trials and tribulations of life. A Southern California transplant, she enjoys anything bright, fluffy, or colorful, as can be seen in her work. When she isn't endeavoring to soak up every ray of sunshine, she works as a freelance designer and illustrator.

Twitter: @tlkateart
Instagram: @thelatestkate
Blog: thelatestkate.tumblr.com
FB: facebook.com/thelatestkate

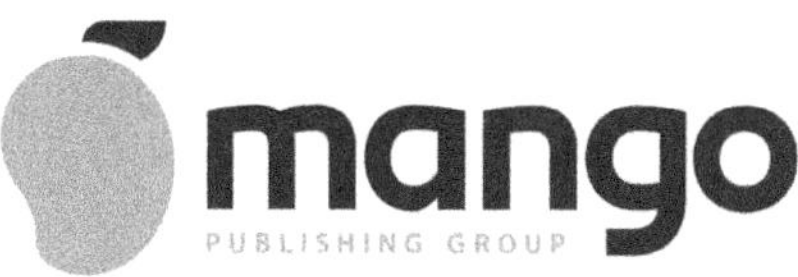

Mango Publishing, established in 2014, publishes an eclectic list of books by diverse authors—both new and established voices—on topics ranging from business, personal growth, women's empowerment, LGBTQ studies, health, and spirituality to history, popular culture, time management, decluttering, lifestyle, mental wellness, aging, and sustainable living. We were recently named 2019 *and* 2020's #1 fastest-growing independent publisher by *Publishers Weekly*. Our success is driven by our main goal, which is to publish high-quality books that will entertain readers as well as make a positive difference in their lives.

Our readers are our most important resource; we value your input, suggestions, and ideas. We'd love to hear from you—after all, we are publishing books for you!

Please stay in touch with us and follow us at:

Facebook: Mango Publishing
Twitter: @MangoPublishing
Instagram: @MangoPublishing
LinkedIn: Mango Publishing
Pinterest: Mango Publishing
Newsletter: mangopublishinggroup.com/newsletter

Join us on Mango's journey to reinvent publishing, one book at a time.

www.ingramcontent.com/pod-product-compliance
Lightning Source LLC
LaVergne TN
LVHW081253100826
845148LV00009B/1209

* 9 7 8 1 6 4 2 5 0 9 1 3 7 *